SELF-ANALYSIS
of
YOUR ORGANIZATION

SELF-ANALYSIS
of
YOUR ORGANIZATION

Seymour L. Rosenberg

A DIVISION OF AMERICAN MANAGEMENT ASSOCIATIONS

Library of Congress Cataloging in Publication Data

Rosenberg, Seymour L
   Self-analysis of your organization.

   1. Decision-making. 2. Management by objectives.
3. Executive ability. I. Title.
HD69.D4R66   658.4   74-75170
ISBN 0-8144-5362-7

© 1974 AMACOM

A division of American Management Associations, New York.

International standard book number: 0-8144-5362-7
Library of Congress catalog card number: 74-75170

First printing

CONTENTS

INTRODUCTION

The most important requirement for the successful operation of a business firm is that its managers have a profound understanding of the nature of their enterprise. This is true because every firm has a nature unique to itself, a set of essential characteristics and patterns of behavior that determines its present performance and its future prospects.

Nevertheless, there is a clear tendency for top-level managers to lose touch with the basic character of their organizations. Rapid company growth, accelerated technological change, and increasing diversification are responsible for this condition. The problem is intensified by the fact that the modern corporation is often in a condition of flux as a result of changes taking place both in the firm and in the social environment that encompasses it.

Corporations have responded to the challenges associated with growth, complexity, and broad diversification by delegating authority and responsibility to powerful and talented operating executives. These chosen leaders, in turn, if they are responsible for complex subunits, also manage by delegation, and so on downward throughout the structure.

As cumbersome as this process may be, no better method has emerged for the management of complex organizations. A significant amount of corporate thinking and planning is devoted to improving and streamlining the process of "management by delegation," or "management by results," in which operating heads at various levels are given great power and authority and are then measured by the results of their performance.

It is important to recognize, however, that this line of management thinking may have dangerous consequences. It is not a far step from the delegation of responsibility from higher to lower management levels to a total dependence on those lower levels. To the extent that higher management focuses on the performance of the operating manager rather than on the dynamics of his organization, top management begins to assume the position of judge rather than manager. As long as the operating executive turns in a good performance, all is well. If he appears to be performing poorly, he can be removed and replaced. Thus the power of management to affect the destiny of the individual operating head is great; however, this is not the same as controlling the destiny of the unit for which he has been given responsibility.

The top management group that falls into the trap of exclusive reliance on operating chiefs and then waits to evaluate their performance is not exercising its management responsibility. Carried to extremes, management by results can easily degenerate into a technique more appropriately described as "management by proconsul." In the days of ancient Rome when its territories were administered by proconsuls, or governors, this technique of governing was, in essence, a primitive version of managing by results. So long as the territory remained pacified, if taxes were collected, if directives were complied with, everything was deemed to be in order. When these criteria were not met, provincial governors were changed. The analogy to modern management by results, when carried to the extremes of total dependency on operating heads, is not too farfetched. Symptomatic of this condition, to complete the analogy, would be total reliance on performance as reported in financial statements and in operating reports measured against planned targets. If the financial statements check out and forecasts are met, all is deemed to be in order. If not, the operating manager sooner or later finds himself in deep trouble, possibly out of a job.

Well, why not? What is so wrong with this idea? And even if it is not perfect, what better method is available to manage the sprawling, complex, modern corporation or corporate division? First of all, the results shown on financial statements are often a reflection of the momentum of previous periods and do not indicate the true current state of the operation or its future prospects. Second, if the reported results are poor, chastising or shuffling operating heads does not necessarily solve the problem that put them in trouble. Third, to manage effectively, business leaders need to identify and correct problems when they are incipient, not after they have become so obvious as to appear on financial statements. Even worse, the top management team that is personality-oriented rather than situation-oriented is often in no position to identify true root causes of poor performance.

Potential consequences to a management team that operates in a free-floating manner above its component organizations, tied to them only by the tenuous thread of operating heads and financial reports, is the development of a condition of disorientation and ultimately of "corporate drift." This happens because a management team, at whatever level, that is not aware of the basic undercurrents that affect the internal life of its suborganizations is not apt to detect on a timely basis signs of loss of vitality or of the blurring of objectives. To keep a business enterprise on course in times of accelerated change requires top-level attention to major factors that influence company performance.

How is this to be accomplished in the complex firm with many suborganizations? The answer is that, even in the most involved organizations, only a handful of critical factors determine the present performance and the future prospects of each profit center. By separating the essential from the nonessential, it is possible for all management levels, from corporate president to manager of the smallest profit center, to focus on these basic characteristics.

In broad outline, these basic characteristics are as follows:

The ability of management, general or local, to cope with change.

The methods employed and the record established in determining and achieving valid objectives.

The nature and the effectiveness of the processes used to arrive at major decisions for change.

The efficiency of the mechanisms utilized to implement such decisions.

The relative strength or weakness of the general decision-making structures in the firm (the decision-command matrix).

The condition of the communications networks and the nature of communication patterns within the firm (are these networks open and free or clogged and deteriorating?).

The personnel profile of the firm (the attention given to maintaining and improving quality levels among personnel).

One last factor associated with those above but also independent of them is the vitality level at which the total organization and its subunits operate—the energy and creativity that determine the driving force of the firm.

These are the indices that define the present condition and determine the future prospects of the business. They are susceptible to analysis and evaluation. When neglected, they tend to deteriorate and to erode the position of the firm, to force it into a state of drift and stagnation. When attended, they are the factors that provide its forward thrust. The job of management at all levels is to understand and control these factors, to counter their strong erosive tendencies, and to stimulate and nurture their constructive possibilities.

There is no general formula that will equip business leaders to understand the basic nature of their firm. This is true because each firm has a background of separate experiences. As a result of the unique nature of each firm, self-knowledge becomes a matter of great importance to the successful conduct of the enterprise. But self-knowledge is not a condition to be arrived at by a simple act of will; it can only be cultivated by a process of continued, disciplined self-appraisal. "Self" is here defined in two ways: the individual manager as he relates to his firm, and the firm as the collective "self."

This book constitutes an attempt to help management develop a systematic program of business self-analysis. The knowledge that can emerge from such a program, consistently applied at all management levels, can be a powerful aid in the difficult business of managing the complex modern enterprise. The discussion that follows is focused on the idea that it is not primarily "new blood" that is required to vitalize the firm in danger of losing direction and momentum, but, rather, a new way for management to look at itself and at the firm that it controls.

1

MANAGEMENT BY PROCONSUL
The Issue in Perspective

The term "management by proconsul" was introduced to describe situations in which management by results as a system of control degenerates into a condition whereby higher levels of management relinquish effective control of their organizations to subordinate managers. The potential for such a tendency to emerge must be recognized, because it is based on powerful objective factors transcending the individual capabilities and intentions of specific managers. The fact is that most high-level business managers are energetic, resourceful, and responsible. They have to be in order to achieve and maintain their positions in publicly held corporations.

The threat to corporate survival that comes from the loss of management control has causes much more profound than the character and personality of individual executives. The trend toward diversification of business lines within the corporate structure, the growing complexity of products and services, and the increasing specialization of function in production, distribution, and marketing are all major challenges to effective top management control.

This is true not only for large, diversified companies but also for relatively homogeneous corporations or corporate divisions. A corporate division head, for instance, has the responsibility for the performance of high-level subordinates who are proficient in disciplines that he does not personally command. Manufacturing, engineering, finance, marketing, and marketing research represent distinct skills, all or some of which are involved in the operation of the relatively complex business enterprise. Not only are these distinct functions, but each of them is in a condition of flux as their individual states of the art improve in response to the demands of a dynamic environment.

GENERALIST VERSUS SPECIALIST

The problem reduces itself to the familiar issue of the generalist, who is responsible for the performance of specialists, who have knowledge in specific areas beyond that of their boss. But this is not the full extent of the issue: for how shall we define the terms "generalist" and "specialist" as applied to an industrial framework? In a managerial sense, at least, a generalist must be classified as an individual who is responsible for areas of activity that are broader and deeper than the scope of his own technical competence. In this context the terms "generalist" and "specialist" become relative, depending on the relationships and positions in the organizational structure. For instance, the head of a diversified company that has a subsidiary that develops and produces aircraft engines is likely to consider the top executive of the subsidiary his specialist in aircraft engines. He, in turn, may have reporting to him, among others, a vice president for engineering. In this relationship, the engine division manager becomes a generalist in relation to the vice president for engineering. The engineering head, in turn, has, let us say, separate directors reporting to him who are in charge of aerodynamics, thermodynamics, metallurgy, and other appropriate disciplines. At this point in terms of our definition, the vice president for engineering takes on the role of generalist with respect to his subordinates.

There are many business organizations, of course, where this interchange of roles does not penetrate so deeply into the reaches of the organizational structure. The extent of this kind of relationship interchange is dependent upon complexity of business line and specialization of function. The point is, however, that in no complex business organization is there any way for the higher managerial levels to operate with full knowledge and understanding of all the specialized functions of their company. In view of these circumstances, it is inevitable that the management of complex organizations should be based upon progressively downward delegation of responsibility and authority throughout the business structure.

However, by justifying the need for extensive downward delegation of responsibility, we resolve no problem; we simply expose a dilemma that plagues complex organizations—namely, leaders of complex organizations cannot be expected to understand in a profound way all the data on which they must base major decisions.

But even this is not the full extent of the problem. Let us take as an example the most complex of organizations in the United States, possibly in the world—the executive branch of our own federal government. The president, on a continuing basis, is compelled to make decisions on economic, social, military, scientific, and many other kinds of issues. Obviously he cannot have the knowledge or the background to make judgments based on the technical merits of each issue. However, let us by a flight of imagination assume that we have a president who is also a superbly qualified technician in all these areas—a great economist, a renowned sociologist, a military expert, a Nobel prize winning physicist. How much better off would the public then be? We know that in each of these areas there are often significant differences of opinion, even among the experts, concerning crucial matters. We have seen that, based on the same data, drastically different conclusions are reached by experts in the same discipline. This is not pointed out in order to minimize the importance of specialized knowledge. It is simply a comment upon the great number of unknowns and variables that are involved in many of the decisions that have to be made at the highest administrative levels.

THE RESPONSIBILITY/KNOWLEDGE PARADOX

The head of an organization, no matter how broad his range of responsibility or how great the resources that he commands, does not have a burden comparable with the awesome one carried by the president of the United States. On a smaller scale, however, his problems in the area of decision making are similar, and the same basic responsibility/knowledge paradox is operative.

There has been no lack of attention given to these inherent problems associated with the management of complex organizations. The general working response has been the evolution of management systems based upon the twin concepts of management by delegation and management by results. Top management divides its complex organization into discrete subunits and employs talented operators to conduct the affairs of each. These managers in turn do the same with respect to their subunits. Then the responsible leaders at each level are measured by the results of their performance against established standards.

DELEGATION AND DEPENDENCY

There is no serious opposition to the idea that the complexity of modern business structures requires the extensive delegation of authority and responsibility. It is pointed out, however, that the inevitable corollary to delegation is dependency. The greater the delegation, the more the dependency. Does this imply that top management is able to fulfill its basic responsibility to control and guide in inverse proportion to the amount of authority and responsibility that it delegates?

Undoubtedly there are powerful factors that can easily bring about the results implied by this question: complexity, diversification, size, all require the downward delegation of authority and responsibility; delegation leads to dependency, and a measure of dependency can lead to total dependency; total dependency inevitably leads to loss of top management control; loss of top management control results in partial or total corporate drift, particularly during periods of rapid change.

THE CRITICAL FACTORS: MEANS TO EFFECTIVENESS

Despite the need for extensive delegation of authority and responsibility in the modern corporation, there is no reason for higher levels of management to relinquish to subordinate levels their basic responsibility to control and guide. There is nothing inevitable about the sequence of conditions described in the previous paragraph. The self-appraisal criteria, or critical factors, discussed in this book provide the basis for effective management control regardless of organizational size or complexity and irrespective of the extent of a firm's delegation system. A manager, at any level, who understands how these factors operate within his organization has the means to fulfill his responsibility, notwithstanding his inability to be expert in each technical and specialized aspect of his function.

The significance of these self-appraisal criteria results from the fact that they have to do with the ongoing processes and basic characteristics that keep the business operative. Consequently, they provide the basis for continuing management attention rather than simply the periodic appraisal of results (the review of performance versus objectives) at artificially (fiscally) established points in time.

It is appropriate here to make an important point concerning these self-appraisal criteria. Each of them is already a potentially fully developed tool. They have been thought about, written about, and debated in academic and practical business circles ever since the rise of the modern corporation. It is our purpose here only to integrate them into a disciplined system of management control by focusing on them as a matrix of coordinated indices. Restated in the form of questions, they demand answers from every level of management. The nature of these answers defines the basic condition of the firm at any given point:

- How do the organization and its subunits establish objectives, and how valid are these objectives?
- How are major decisions for change arrived at?
- How are these decisions implemented?
- How does the ongoing decision-making apparatus in the organization function?
- How effective is the communications process?

- How powerful is the basic life force that drives the organization?

It is reemphasized that this kind of management focus is not proposed as an alternative to management by results. On the contrary, it provides a method for preventing delegation systems from degenerating into total dependency systems. This can be done because the self-appraisal criteria provide for a clear understanding of results, as opposed to a simple measurement of results against targets or standards. In addition, higher management levels are placed in a position where they may make independent and informed evaluations of submitted "variance explanations." Finally, since these criteria are process-oriented rather than after-the-fact event-oriented, they provide the basis for early warning information. They accomplish this by making it possible to identify problems while they are still incipient rather than when they surface in the form of quantifiable results.

The thrust of this chapter so far has been that there are tools available to bridge the gap between responsible top-level management and its antithesis, management by proconsul, notwithstanding the difficulties presented by size, complexity, diversification, and specialization of function. The self-appraisal factors described here have been identified as such tools. But to have a true understanding of these factors (or criteria or indices) as they pertain to a particular firm, the management team must be prepared to look inward to the basic nature of its organization. It must become committed to the idea of corporate or organizational introspection. It must understand the need to strengthen its links with its operating units without smothering them with controls and interferences. It must also understand that the critical factors have negative aspects that in certain circumstances can work against, rather than support, the firm.

THE EROSIVE FACTORS: FORCES AGAINST THE FIRM

It was suggested in the Introduction that when neglected, the critical factors that determine the relative well-being of the firm tend to deteriorate and to erode its position. We shall here further explain this idea by discussing the forces that work against the interests of the firm when not kept under close management control. The discussion divides itself naturally into two parts: the first concerns those factors that relate to the internal dynamics of the firm; the second deals with those that have to do with the relationship of the company with its surrounding environment. An understanding of these erosive aspects is an important step in helping management to achieve a condition of corporate introspection.

The Internal Erosive Factors

Dependency on past success patterns: A general problem

Business organizations, like individuals, have a tendency to become set in their ways as they grow older. As time passes in the life of a firm, it accumulates experiences that enter into its collective memory. Unsuccessful ventures, ideas, approaches, formulas, and ways of doing business are discarded or repressed. The successful experiences are likely to remain in the company's memory bank, ready for immediate recall and use. They form the basis for the firm's policies, procedures, and business approaches. As the company grows in importance and advances in age, there is, therefore, a tendency increasingly to rely on the old, proven ways of doing business. This is not unreasonable. Solid past experience, after all, should lay the basis for successful future experiences.

These are obvious truths that no reasonable individual is likely to deny. However, essentially because of their validity, they carry with them certain dangerous corollaries. Consider this. To the extent that a firm believes it has a set of successful formulas to rely on, it has less apparent need or stimulus for independent thought regarding the present and, to some degree, even the future. The managers who have developed the successful old approaches may feel no need to look for new ones. Why increase the uncertainties in an already uncertain world? Why look for new truths when old ones stand out like beacons in a troubled sea?

Such attitudes, understandable as they may be, inevitably have a residual impact throughout the ranks of middle and lower management. If the company with its proven record of accomplishment is disposed to place heavy emphasis on past experience, the creative drive at middle and lower management levels is likely to atrophy because of limited opportunity. The enthusiasm and the drive to innovate among working management people cannot long survive the frustration of their finding themselves always stymied by references to previous experience—good or bad. For creative management people, this kind of environment leaves only the alternatives of get out or give up and conform. If a firm thinks it is really programmed for success, then there is little apparent further need for the creative, innovative manager. If such a situation were actually to exist in a company, that is, the availability of a programmed answer for most questions, then the need in terms of management talent would be more for the conformist, who will successfully use existing programs, than for the innovator.

It may seem to be a paradox, but specifically those firms which have been most successful must face the danger that their management cadres will be subject to an almost imperceptible weakening of the creative drive that in some earlier period gave to the firm its ability to grow and to prosper. It should be recognized that it is the maturing, successful company that is most likely, in many circumstances, to lose the flexibility of its management thinking. In these times of rapid change, particularly, such loss of flexibility represents a real danger.

There is no single, simple solution to the problems associated with loss of flexibility in the maturing firm. Clearly, however, the first step in counteracting this tendency is to become aware of it. The propensity to lose flexibility and freshness in management thinking can be best combated by a thoughtful, aware management team continually striving to strike a proper balance between experience and innovation. This balance can be achieved by reviewing the basic factors, the self-appraisal criteria, that measure the condition of the firm.

Diffusion of company objectives

When a firm is young, management knows why the company was formed, what hopes it has for it, and what its objectives are. However, with the passage of time, changing conditions often force changes from original objectives. As the company grows, new personnel join the firm and new goals are added to or are substituted for old ones. The higher levels of management are broadened and deepened; new and separate points of view enter the firm. With the increasing complexity of the business environment, the future becomes more clouded and uncertain, and differing opinions evolve concerning the best course for the company to follow. Objectives become more difficult to define.

There is, therefore, a real danger that without being fully aware of it a company can be approaching a state of drift, a condition in which it operates on the momentum generated in previous periods, without the benefit of clear objectives for the future. It is very easy for such a situation to come about gradually. How is management to ascertain whether it has arrived at such a condition? And once the problem is recognized, how is it to be dealt with? These are questions that require periodic asking. Honest, valid answers can only come through the process of continual self-appraisal.

Decision making for an uncertain future

An important aspect of decision making and decision implementation in a firm are the major decisions for change that every high-level executive must make as part of his job. These decisions may involve significant commitments of resources, major organizational realignments, risky pricing formulas, or any one of the numerous other possible steps management takes that can have far-reaching consequences for the prospects of the company. In these times, when the shape of the future is becoming increasingly indistinct, how are such decisions made in the firm? How does the top-level executive face the challenge of having to commit irretrievable resources to a future that is likely to be unprecedented in terms of its rate and direction of change? Are the methods used to make and to implement major decisions adequate for the formidable environment in which they must take place; or is the decision-making process becoming increasingly arbitrary and subjective?

Degradation of the decision matrix

As a firm matures both planned and unplanned changes are bound to take place in the decision-making process. The larger and more complex the company becomes, the more diffuse and less controllable becomes the process of making decisions. In a company employing 30 people, the employer can decide when overtime is to be worked and whether it is really required. Who makes these decisions in the 3,000-person unit? And what are the bases on which they are made? At what level are make or buy decisions made in a manufacturing firm, and what are the criteria for arriving at them? These are examples of routine but significant decisions that must be made on a continuing basis in a going enterprise. Unless management carefully and systematically appraises its actual current decision-making practices as compared with its theoretical policies, major areas of decision making may be lost to the control of the firm's leaders. The natural tendency is for the decision-making process to be grasped by the "man on the spot." Unless carefully controlled, the result can be a tangle of uncoordinated, contradictory company actions that are contrary to the well-being of the firm.

Weakening of communication channels

A major factor that works against the interest of the company as it grows and matures lies in the tendency of communication patterns to lag behind in adjusting to changes in company structure that occur during periods of internal growth or growth through acquisitions. Communication channels in a business firm may be likened to the nervous system of advanced living organisms: when the nervous system of a living species is no longer adequate to deal with the changing environment, either the species adapts or it becomes extinct. The analogy between this biological phenomenon and the rapidly growing, modern corporation is striking. Management levels in the increasingly complex business organizations of today require inputs from remote sources of information. The remoteness may or may not be geographical, but it is certainly hierarchical. In turn, the farthest corners of the corporate structure must receive and *properly understand* the communications conveyed from the higher levels within the business structure. It is clear that as a business expands, communications processes become more precarious: the owner of a 30-person business can feel more confident that he knows what is happening in his firm from day to day than the head of a business structure with 3,000 or 30,000 people.

Remoteness and size, however, are not the only obstacles to communication in the modern business enterprise. Individuals sitting in neighboring offices may have their own communications gaps: a general manager vis-à-vis his staff; staff members among themselves; a staff member with his subordinates. This kind of gap is perhaps the most serious communications problem that can befall the modern corporation.

For all of these reasons, the pattern of communications in the firm requires close monitoring for any signs of deterioration.

Loss of touch with internal change:
The changing personnel profile

Another area that requires close management attention has to do with the changes that continually take place among the firm's personnel and in the character of their mutual relationships.

In some situations, the changes are rapid and striking, such as the infusion of new employees to accommodate a condition of quick personnel turnover or a situation of rapid growth. The impact of such changes is immediately felt.

There are other personnel-related changes, however, that because of their slow, natural pace do not force themselves on the attention of management. An example of this is the normal aging process of human beings. What is the impact on a company, for instance, of a stable middle management group whose average age and length of service keep increasing? Or, what sort of changes in business attitudes and approaches are brought about by normal, unaccelerated personnel turnover? Men are shaped by their previous experience. Is the sum total of new experiences being brought into the firm by new personnel as valuable as the sum total of the experience being drained from it by departing personnel? Or another example of the changing personnel profile—how does the average management trainee, newly graduated from school and now entering the company, compare with his counterpart of five years ago or ten years ago? Is the same training program still as useful and relevant for the current trainee as was formulated for the trainee of yesterday? The life-styles and attitudes of today's college graduate are quite different from those of just a short decade ago. What impact is this having on the firm?

In the preceding paragraphs, we have been dealing essentially with changes within and among salaried personnel. Equally important, however, are the changes in nature and attitude among hourly employees, those already in the labor force as well as those about to enter.

For those companies which deal with their hourly employees through labor union representation, the trend of management-union relations is of great significance to the future of the firm. How much attention is given to analyzing the status of this relationship before the time comes to negotiate new management-union contracts? For instance, it is important to understand the current thinking and feelings of the hourly employee with respect to his loyalty images. Does he identify his interests with the interests of the company notwithstanding his union allegiance? Or does the union stand as a wall between long-run company objectives and the hourly laborer? Without constant attention, there is a strong likelihood that the relationship between management and organized labor in any given firm will deteriorate, as a result of a lack of understanding of the actual dynamics involved in the relationship as opposed to images that management may be carrying over from the past.

Each of these issues has a significant bearing on the company's "psychic energy" level, the level of creativity and drive that provides the firm with its forward thrust. The management that is not acutely conscious of this elusive aspect of company performance may find too late that its organization is losing ground in the struggle for survival in a changing environment.

The External Erosive Factors

There are also factors outside its environment that have immediate and direct relevance to the company's well-being. The main outside influences on the firm are those which occur in the marketplace among the customers and potential customers of the company and those which take place as a result of the fiscal and monetary policy of the federal government. These factors have an integral and direct bearing on the objectives of the firm and require close attention.

Market-related changes

The greatest calamity that can befall a business firm is for it to lose its market. When a company loses its market, it has lost its economic and social reason for existence. During the decade of the 1970s, three kinds of change will pose a continual threat to the viability of business firms that sell commodities or services.

Technological change. The first of these, technological change, is not new, and by and large the American industrial community has both stimulated it and evolved techniques to cope with its dislocating impacts. It is, nevertheless, not to be assumed that either the talent or the drive to bring about technological change is a permanent or self-perpetuating trait. When the readiness to invest in research and development on a risk basis and the spirit of innovation begin to falter in industrial enterprises, past technological successes become matters only of historical interest.

Changes in buyer attitudes. There are clear signs that we are now at the beginning of a period when a life-style-conscious population will be redefining its concept of needs, wants, and luxuries. In the past, the advertising industry, through the use of the media, has largely molded the pattern of effective demand in this country. This has been true across the board, from cereals to toothpaste, to ladies' wear, to automobiles and motorcycles. The programming of consumer tastes by market suppliers is now clearly in jeopardy. And that which affects consumer industries ultimately affects the vendors to consumer industries, such as capital goods producers.

The government as customer. These days it is generally accepted that the government of the United States plays a critical role in determining both the level and the direction of economic activity in the country. The public sector of the economy is merely another name for the government as customer. The requirements of this customer are determined by both national and international considerations, by economic necessities, and by political and social pressures. There has been an intensive debate among the population concerning the need to reorder the country's priorities. There has been a growing demand for greater public expenditures in the area of pollution control, economic advancement of the poor, and better quality education. For the economist, reordering of priorities means reallocation of resources. For American industry, it means drastic changes in the pattern of demand for goods and services.

For the self-aware company, all three market-related factors—technological change, life-style change, reordering of national priorities—raise the question "How must we change to protect our position as a supplier of goods and services during the coming decade?"

Changes in government fiscal and monetary policy

Aside from the government's control over a significant portion of the nation's purchasing power (a factor that has been defined as market-related), the government has the power to manipulate the federal tax structure, that is, to exercise fiscal policies and to influence the cost of and availability of money in the economy, that is, to exercise monetary policies. In times of recession, the government may move to take fiscal and monetary measures to stimulate the economy. In times of full or near full utilization of resources, it may take actions in a counter direction in order to cool off the economy. For the individual firm, serious questions arise concerning the relationship between government economic policy at any given time and the well-being of the enterprise. Some government policies have an impact that the individual company cannot influence, such as changes in the money supply. Other policies are directly aimed at the individual firm; such as the investment tax credit. These policies, although implemented in fulfillment of government plans and strategies of the day, have long-run influences on the life of the individual firm.

How well is the individual firm, how well is your company, equipped to analyze the short-run and long-run impacts of government economic policy as it affects the company operation? Does the company react to changes in government fiscal and monetary policy on an opportunistic basis, or does it measure these changes from the perspective of fundamental company objectives?

DIFFICULTIES OF SELF-APPRAISAL

Upon reflection, the importance of introducing the idea of organizational introspection or self-appraisal into the business as a continuing discipline should become readily apparent. The real issue, however, is that it is not easy for individuals or for groups to enter into such a process in a meaningful way. There are substantial obstacles that must be overcome by a business management before it can successfully undertake the process of self-appraisal, either together as a collective team or separately as individual managers. The major obstacles are the pressures of day-to-day responsibility; the natural reluctance to face hard truths; the trap of in-group thinking; fear of rocking the boat; and modern life-style distractions. These obstacles are not insurmountable; but if they are to be overcome, they must be set forth, understood, and placed in perspective.

Pressures of Day-to-Day Responsibility

The most constructive and dynamic individuals in the management group are likely to be its busiest and most preoccupied managers. The responsibility for dealing with the problems of the hour, the day, and the week and for making on-the-spot decisions concerning current business issues normally gravitates to those with the temperament and the vitality within the organization to cope with such matters. Whatever their position, these are the natural leaders, the contributors. Since the most valuable managers are usually enmeshed in the problems of today, they ordinarily have little time or patience for the kind of self-appraisal that provides perspective to deal with the issues of tomorrow until those issues become current in the form of problems, perhaps of major proportions.

Indeed, even if the preoccupied executive has the insight to recognize the signs of future problems, he has a ready-made mechanism to put off dealing with them, particularly if they involve unpleasant or difficult decisions. He has only to immerse himself still further in his current workload, thus deferring, with a semblance of legitimacy, issues that do not appear to require immediate attention. In this way the busy manager can continue to draw satisfaction from the idea that he is dealing in a highly efficient manner with the matters that are continually coming across his desk, while the future with its problems recedes from his daily consciousness. By his neglect of tomorrow's issues, the manager in effect creates his workload for the future. But few of tomorrow's problems can be dealt with by improvising, even by a brilliant improviser. Business firms rushing into the future like cars speeding along unknown roads cannot stop on the dime and change direction to avoid impending disaster.

All of this points to one simple conclusion. The modern business manager, immersed as he is in the task of doing his share to keep his organization functioning on a continuing basis, needs to discover how to step back and perceive the total situation. He has to find a way of developing a sense of perspective that will integrate the total condition of his organization—where it has been, where it is, and where it is heading.

Reluctance to Face Hard Truths

Self-esteem is essential to the morale of both individuals and collective social groups. In the abrasive environment in which most of us function, events and experiences abound that tend to have a negative effect on our self-esteem: errors of various sorts, regretted acts of meanness or pettiness, poor decisions, mistaken judgments, past acts of omission or commission. Fortunately, we also have the capacity to submerge or to rationalize negative events and experiences. This is a necessary trait for the individual functioning in our society, since to function effectively, we must each of us have some measure of self-esteem. To the extent that we do not have to bear the full weight of our failures on a day-to-day basis, our capacity to think well of ourselves is enhanced.

What is true of the individual is also true of the collective, if only because collectives are made up ultimately of individuals. There is a self-protective tendency for groups, as well, to submerge or rationalize bad experiences and to remember and cherish good ones. This is one of the obstacles in the way of achieving a pattern of honest self-appraisal. If a business management group is to probe its own actions, it must risk bringing out bad individual or collective experiences; for whereas it is true that the capacity to cushion oneself against negative experiences is often constructive, this capacity can also lead to disastrous, long-term effects.

It is not only the bitterness of having to deal with unpleas-antness that is an obstacle to seeking the truth in a situation; there is also the eventuality to be faced that an honest analysis of a set of business circumstances may lead to conclusions that will require difficult, disagreeable decisions. So long as problems are not defined and pursued to their conclusion, so long as issues are not clarified, there will always be excuses for inaction. Very often a real understanding of the issues facing a company com-pels implementation of actions unpleasant to think about, with far-reaching consequences for individuals and groups within the firm.

The Trap of In-Group Thinking

Individuals who work in close proximity, as is the case with management groups, tend broadly to reinforce each other's views and ideas. Even if the group is constituted of persons with a high level of intelligence, independence, and individuality, the normal tendency is for consensus. Even when differences of opinion and viewpoint emerge, the range of discussion and debate is bounded by the disparate ideas that emerge from the group itself. This means that no matter how vigorous a discussion may be, it is limited to the views put forth by the actual participants. Grad-ually, therefore, over a period of time an invisible fence is built, restricting the outermost limits of intellectual exploration to the frame of reference within which the group operates. For this reason, management groups attuned to the idea of self-appraisal must find ways to break out of the boundaries set by their own ideas and preconceptions. Recognition of this inherent obstacle to creative, innovative thinking is the first requirement for escap-ing the confines of in-group thinking. Whenever possible, there-fore, it is important to expose the premises and preconceptions of the group itself to outside challenges.

Fear of Rocking the Boat

It is the unusual leadership group that does not harbor among its personnel patterns of personality conflict, incompatible personal ambitions, or some feelings of individual vulnerability. Among a dynamic group of responsible managers operating in the difficult, often abrasive environment of modern business, it is understandable that such conditions should develop. The unacceptability of uncivil behavior, the need to get on with the job, and the unpredictable results of open clashes usually serve to keep personal differences submerged. Often, however, this surface equilibrium is precarious. A particular action, an expressed criticism, or a harsh comment by a member of the "team" may upset the delicate balance. The expression "don't rock the boat" defines an attitude designed to maintain relationships in equilibrium, notwithstanding the fact that it may be important to bring particular issues to the surface. It should be recognized that the process of self-appraisal within a management group carries with it the possibility that from time to time the boat may *have* to be rocked.

It is clear that honest self-appraisal on an individual basis or on a group level may turn out, at least in the beginning, to be a painful process. Personal feelings of insecurity may emerge, misunderstandings of motives may take place, submerged antagonisms may surface. There is no point in minimizing the possibility of such reactions. It is a simple fact that any true process of introspection requires a level of individual and group maturity capable of withstanding the strains imposed by the process. For the business organization, this means that self-appraisal must focus on issues and that personality involvements must be de-emphasized. In other words, the introspection process must be analytical and objective, not critical and judgmental.

Life-Style Distractions

There are many obstacles to self-appraisal that face the management group as a whole and the manager as an individual during the course of the business day. But how about the management person when he leaves the hectic environment of his business office? What happens when he enters the peace and calm of his home and the circle of his family and friends? Why can he not sit before his fireplace, put into perspective the events of the day, and mull over the "big picture" as it affects his company? One quick answer to these questions is that many business executives carry home with them briefcases full of work that must be done during the evening hours just to stay even with the job's requirements and do justice to their responsibilities.

One may or may not view with a measure of skepticism this picture of the typical executive poring over his work papers till the late hours. There are, however, other cogent reasons that make it difficult for him to place in perspective during evening hours the overall condition of his business unit. It should be recognized that the life-style and living environment of many of today's business leaders impose pressures on them that begin when they open their eyes in the morning and continue until they fall asleep at night, lingering perhaps even while they sleep. When he comes home at night after having spent his most creative and alert hours at work, the business manager, if he is to be a successful husband and father, must make an effort to shake off the day's concerns, impressions, and aggravations and somehow reidentify with the interests of his other important worlds—his family and perhaps his community. He must be prepared to identify with the problems placed before him by his wife, he must make a valiant effort to bridge the generation gap between himself and his children. Outside the home, he may be the man counted on to bring the community fund campaign over the top.

All of this is not to say that the business executive succeeds in any or all of these extra work obligations. However, irrespective of his relative success or failure, the pressures and preoccupations of life outside the firm are there to be faced. It is for another book and another writer to probe deeper into these issues. The fact remains that there is an overwhelming tendency for the life-style of the business executive not to be conducive to development of an attitude of introspection and self-appraisal, with respect either to his business life or to his personal and community lives.

The obstacles to corporate introspection and self-appraisal by individual managers and management groups are the result of conditions deeply rooted in the social and business environment. Each distracting influence, together with the increasing complexity of corporate life, contributes to a tendency toward fragmented perceptions rather than perceptions that integrate and unify.

The antidote to distraction is focus. By keeping in clear view those factors that ultimately influence the performance of his organization, the business manager is enabled to separate the essential from the nonessential, the important from the trivial. By directing his attention to fundamentals (described in this book as the critical factors), he can make best use of his most valuable, but inherently limited, personal resources: ability, time, and energy. This is true both for the individual manager and for total management teams. It is especially true during the times of trouble, confusion, and disorientation that are often brought about by rapid or sudden change. But regardless of the severity of circumstances, an understanding of and attention to fundamentals will provide a basic frame of reference for the restoration of individual and group equilibrium.

The chapters that follow bring into focus, one by one, the critical factors that determine the condition of the firm. They are worth repeating here at the outset: the company's approach to setting objectives, the way it initiates decisions for change, the way it implements them, how operating decisions are made and who makes them, the firm's communication patterns, and the general vitality level at which the business and its component parts operate.

2

OBJECTIVES OF THE FIRM

Most publicly owned business firms, large and diversified or small and homogeneous, share a common goal: to utilize their resources in a manner that will provide the maximum possible return on those resources and at the same time be compatible with the long-term, best interests of the company. This ultimate objective is an abstraction, no more than a wish or a hope, for there is nothing self-fulfilling about such a goal. To finally accomplish it, to convert it into a reality, a firm must first have a set of specific implementing objectives. This is true whether the firm is large, with many profit centers, or small, consisting of one or only a few profit centers.

When a firm has decided upon the precise nature of the business lines, product lines, products, or services that it wishes to make available to the marketplace for the immediate and intermediate future periods, it has a clear basis for the establishment of specific objectives. These objectives have to do with when, where, and how the firm plans to bring to market its defined products or services; they are also related to the operating conditions required to keep the company competitive.

A firm or a profit center that has doubts about the future

market potential of its products or services because of changing market conditions, but which clearly recognizes its predicament, also has a basis for establishing a set of specific objectives.

For a given organization with established products or services unthreatened by obsolescence, the objectives might be:

1. To increase its market share by a specific percentage by a given time through expansion into a new geographical area with the aid of an extensive marketing program and an expanded distribution system.

2. To maintain its present highly satisfactory position in its current market area by improving customer services in order to maintain customer loyalty.

3. To intensify its product improvement program and to introduce further operating efficiencies in order to extend into the future its present strong business position.

The organization that is faced with the threat of total product or service obsolescence would require a completely different set of top priority objectives, perhaps similar to the following:

1. To conduct a search for a new set of products or services that is compatible with the firm's basic capabilities and resources.

2. To launch a capital conservation effort as a means of gathering the resources needed to implement new programs.

The two sets of objectives described above pertain to firms with obviously different circumstances. The first set of objectives relates to a business organization preparing itself for further growth and increased profitability. The second set pertains to a firm fighting for its very existence. Yet despite these basic differences, both situations identify organizations with one fundamental thing in common: a sense of awareness, an understanding of the direction in which they must move.

THE DRIFTING FIRM

A company that is operating without a clear idea of what it should be bringing to the marketplace in the near and intermediate futures, or one that is uncertain about how to sell its products or services and is doing little or nothing to correct the situation, has either approached or is approaching a state of drift. It is likely that the resources of a company operating in either condition are being wastefully diffused and dissipated. It is also likely that the key personnel of such a company are working at cross purposes for lack of direction. Still worse, the possibility exists that the top men of the affected firm or profit center are operating on a reflexive, habitual level, depending on the momentum of previous, more productive periods, doing the best they can to disguise their basic feelings of helplessness and resignation. Worst of all, the affected executives might be deceiving themselves completely about the true state of their organization.

Possibilities for Self-Deception

Of all the problems that the modern business firm may encounter, loss of sense of direction is the most profound. This is true because it raises questions concerning the enterprise's very reason to exist.

It is important to recognize in this connection that one of the great talents of human beings as individuals and in groups is a propensity for self-deception. The areas of business planning and business objectives are particularly susceptible to self-deception because the subject matter has to do with the future. And in dealing with the future, the persuasiveness of business rhetoric can be overpowering not only to outsiders but to insiders as well. It is understandable, therefore, how a particular management group might easily dismiss or minimize the extent of those problems that relate to the future.

Business planning documents are an example of the persuasiveness of unsubstantiated rhetoric when applied to the future. There is something inherently appealing about a planning document that depicts a promising future. It is probably not too broad a generalization to say that a set of pessimistic planning projections is more likely to provoke the analytical attention and capabilities of management than a set of optimistic ones. Yet the only requirements for the preparation of an optimistic planning document are a gift for language, an understanding of general planning techniques, and some comprehension of the business environment.

The planning department of any firm can prepare a broad

set of projections containing a large amount of valid background material even though no one in the company, least of all the planners, has the slightest idea of how the projections are to be converted to reality. To the stymied management group, whose company or profit center is losing its sense of direction but who is unwilling or unable to recognize the predicament, a set of such documents may offer false reassurance. This may be the case even if nothing is taking place in the firm's day-to-day activity to indicate that the projections are in the process of being converted to reality.

The Difficulty of Choosing Objectives

It is not simply because of management incompetence or negligence that business firms lose their sense of direction. If the issue of management objectives is to be honestly dealt with, it must be recognized that there is no easy way for a management group to assure itself of keeping its enterprise on course from year to year and decade to decade. There are fundamental problems deeply rooted in the nature and dynamics of industrial societies that make this issue unresponsive to simple, formula-type solutions.

Well-defined objectives, which are necessary to achieve clear direction, are not always easy to establish or to maintain in a time of increasing social, economic, and technological change. Not only is the rate of change accelerating, but, even more important, the directions of change are often not clear insofar as they affect the objectives of individual industries. Less than a quarter of a century ago, reciprocating engines for large aircraft provided the basis for a thriving industry. Today the major supplier of such engines is no longer a factor in the aircraft engine business.

Another example indicative of creeping obsolescence is the accelerated trend toward miniaturization of electronic components, mainly through the introduction of integrated circuitry. This development is making obsolete whole sections of the electronic components business.

Still another example is the case of the automobile engine. These days manufacturers of internal combustion engines and engine components are facing the threat of obsolescence as a result of the search for nonpolluting automobile power plants.

These are a few examples of the impact of new technologies and changing values on industries that only recently believed they were on course, in pursuit of valid objectives. It is not surprising, therefore, to find that the rapid approach of obsolescence should leave the affected management groups disoriented and perhaps not fully organized to cope with their predicaments.

To tell experienced business leaders that they should have valid objectives for their enterprises is akin to explaining addition and subtraction to skilled mathematicians. There is no controversy among management people concerning the idea that the establishment and pursuit of clear objectives is a major function of business leadership. The problem arises as a result of the implementing decisions that are required to accomplish these objectives.

Viewed from this perspective, the issue of corporate disorientation with respect to objectives takes on another dimension. Consider the fact that the implementation of revised company objectives and plans requires a commitment of long-term resources that have relatively little transferability and liquidity. In an environment of incomplete and uncertain visibility, to run the risk of making irrevocable choices through the commitment of irretrievable resources may often appear more dangerous than simply to make no significant decisions for change, particularly if the enterprise is in a position to continue for a while propelled by the momentum of previous periods.

Risk of Change Versus Risk of Inaction

There is no easy answer to the problem of committing irretrievable resources to new objectives in an uncertain environment. However, one significant fact should be recognized by management groups faced with this dilemma. Although it may seem easier to delay making decisions in the face of an unclear future, it is not necessarily safer. To put off making a decision is in itself an important decision. It is an illusion to think otherwise. If the absence of decision leads to company obsolescence, the consequences may be far more drastic than risk commitments based upon the anticipated demands of the future. This is true because management inaction in the face of approaching obsolescence presents the alternative of almost certain disaster. On the other hand, reorientation of objectives and reallocation of resources represent the kinds of risk that are normal in today's business environment and offer at least average opportunities for average success.

EVALUATING THE OBJECTIVES

The most painful aspect of a company's loss of direction is the need to confront the fact that clear objectives are no longer in view. For a management group, this condition is akin to that of a person who has lost his sense of purpose and consequently, perhaps, his sense of worth. The psychological barriers to acknowledging such a condition, either for individuals or for groups, are considerable. Nevertheless, at some level of consciousness every management group knows when it is in serious trouble from the standpoint of future objectives—even when it has yielded to the temptation to ignore or to minimize the problem. This is a temptation that needs to be overcome, because recognition of the existence of a condition of drift is the first step to its correction. It is, therefore, of major importance that business managements cultivate the habit of honest self-appraisal concerning the status of their objectives.

How are management groups to become involved in such a process? The answer is that specific criteria are available to corporate and profit-center managements to determine the status of organizational objectives. By use of these criteria, even the management of a complex corporation with multiple profit centers can evaluate both its own overall objectives and those of its individual centers. An individual profit center or a smaller corporation, of course, is even better able to conduct such an appraisal or investigation.

The management group that has the courage (and perhaps the humility) to ask itself, "Do we really have a set of objectives?" and "How firmly do we really believe in our objectives?" can find the answers close at hand, by careful analysis of the firm's planning documents and by a comparison of daily "real life" in the firm as compared to the company plans, evaluating the actual pattern of resource use in the organization.

The Company Plan as a Test of Objectives

The accomplishment of an organization's business objectives comes about as a result of definite, purposeful actions aimed at achieving those objectives. If the activities and the events, or milestones, required for the fulfillment of objectives are clearly defined and programmed, first indications are that the organization knows where it wants to go and how it intends to get there. Consequently, in order to be meaningful, the plan should be a detailed scenario of what must take place to accomplish the objectives of the firm. If the planning documents are general in nature and in no place describe a definite course of action, there is reason to believe that the organization is not being prepared to implement objectives. This may be because management does not know what specific course of action to take, though it might have some general ideas. Here, for example, are hypothetical abstracts representing two different approaches to the preparation of planning papers. Each deals with future market definition and associated investment requirements:

1. *General plan.* ". . . Historically, our firm has succeeded in capturing between 5 percent and 10 percent of the regional market for our product line. During the past three years, our sales share has been closer to the lower end of this range. However, by instituting a vigorous product improvement program, upgrading our facilities, and waging a more aggressive advertising campaign, we should at least approach the upper end of the range. Our 15-year historical trend based on a 'line of best fit' indicates that 8 percent of the market share should be ours at the end of the next two years, when we project this trend into the future."

2. *Specific plan.* ". . . It has been a source of considerable concern to management that our market share has been declining during the past three years notwithstanding a longer-term trend that indicates that it should be increasing. Management has concluded that the success enjoyed in previous periods has led the

company to take its market position for granted and to delay the implementation of required product innovations. The decline in the company's market share is clearly a result of the fact that we have allowed our products to lag behind those of our more aggressive competitors.

"To correct the situation, we have instituted product improvement plans, which are now in the design stage. Our milestone schedules indicate that we should be in the market with an improved product line in two years, enabling us to recapture our share of the market by the end of three years. A complete study has been made of the equipment and tooling that will be required for our product-line innovations. Equipment lists have been drawn up and purchase lead times have been calculated. Cash flow projections have been prepared, and management has authority to commit the necessary resources required to restore our market position. The remainder of this section describes the plan of action, including a schedule of activities and events that will enable us to achieve our business objective. . . ."

The two hypothetical plan extracts describe different responses to the same problem—the threat of product-line obsolescence. Each plan indicates an awareness of the problem. Both plans agree about the right general solution to the problem. Both even project corrective actions.

The first extract, however, gives no indication of how the issue is actually to be resolved except in general terms. It projects a hope for better days ahead without describing what commitments are to be made in order to make this hope a reality. It does not describe a new product configuration. It raises no questions concerning the resources or facilities that will be required to accomplish the product improvement goal. If this hypothetical extract were indicative of the total extent of management thinking about the future, it would suggest a firm without clear objectives despite apparent recognition of major problems. To define the problem and offer the obvious general solution without the accompanying program of action is merely an exercise in rhetoric rather than a plan to accomplish objectives.

The second hypothetical extract defines a firm with a clear idea of the course of action it plans to take. It has already committed itself in terms of the required resources. It has established a program of action with time-related milestones. It has prepared a scenario of future activities and events.

However, even the existence of a set of apparently clear objectives and a well-defined plan is not of itself proof that an enterprise is operating with a sense of direction. There must also be a demonstrated readiness to commit company resources to fulfill the requirements of the plan. Otherwise the firm's detailed plans may still be little more than a set of props to keep management from facing the truth that it is really operating without direction. There may be little relationship between the planning data, detailed as they may be, and what is actually taking place in the company's day-to-day operation.

Nevertheless, the first test of company objectives is the company plan. Let us further consider this aspect before moving to others. For if the company plan fails this test, it is almost certain that other criteria will substantiate the failure.

Reviewing the company plan

The period during which management reviews its annual forecasts presents the best opportunity for appraising the firmness of its objectives. Normally, such a review covers not only the coming fiscal year but also the longer-range future. (How far ahead the projections extend depends upon the nature of the industry within which the enterprise functions. Different industries have different natural visibilities. A utility, for instance, has greater visibility than a clothing firm. On the other hand, its required lead times for commitments are also far greater. It therefore can, and must, plan much farther ahead.)

The corporate management of a multiprofit-center enterprise has a more complex task in reviewing plans and objectives than does the management of a single-profit-center organization. Not only must the plans and objectives of the individual profit centers be appraised, but those of the overall corporation require the same analysis. The validity and the feasibility of each individual plan must be probed. The conviction behind each plan must be evaluated. In addition, top management must be prepared to measure its own capability and willingness to support the plans of the individual profit centers. Incompatible projects must be eliminated. Plans that require more resources than top management is able or willing to underwrite must be weeded out.

The review period should be a time of questioning, a time for overall corporate introspection. This is especially important for the management of multiprofit-center firms that operate with a philosophy of decentralization and significant profit-center autonomy. For such organizations, once the guidelines are set, the individual profit-center operators will be off and running. The difference between real dialogue and slipshod review at this crucial time may determine whether the profit-center manager will operate as an autonomous leader with strong ties to corporation management or as a proconsul on his own to be judged only when the results are in.

The review of profit-center plans and projections presents a major opportunity for corporate management to gain an understanding of the nature of its firm. This is obviously true for the relatively small or homogeneous company. It is also true for the complex firm with many profit centers, even if these are diverse in nature. In addition to establishing first indications about the firmness and validity of profit-center objectives, the individual plans should also offer a basis for understanding the anatomy, the nuts-and-bolts aspect, of each individual unit.

How is such an understanding to be achieved? The answer is that top management must focus on essentials. By requiring that profit-center planning documents address themselves to basic issues in specific terms, management can make its difficult task of achieving an overall perspective much more manageable.

What are the essentials that top management should focus on during plan-review sessions? They are basically the following: the profitability and projected life span of current products, the new products that are being programmed for the future, the present and future cash requirements of the profit centers to accomplish stated objectives, sales and profit projections by product, return-on-investment projections.

The current product mix. It is clear that profit-center management must have a detailed grasp of the market potential of its current product mix, with respect to both profitability and longevity. It is equally necessary for overall corporate management to have the same grasp. This can be accomplished by management's demanding a mature, realistic appraisal of future problems and prospects from the profit center. During plan-review sessions these should be realistically presented and discussed. Unsubstantiated rhetoric should be challenged. Market projections should be compared with independent data, which is often available from government or industrial sources in concise and inexpensive form.

New products. The threat of product obsolescence is a constant specter in the current economic and social environment. Profit-center planning to meet this threat should be a vital concern to corporate management. A major test of subunit objectives is the concreteness of such planning. Are new-product configurations completely defined? (If the firm is a service enterprise, the same criterion would apply. For instance, a new product in an insurance company might be a variable-annuity insurance policy designed to meet changing economic conditions. Such a product, too, must be designed and tested.) In the case of either tangible or intangible products, does the plan contain a total scenario of activities and events from design to method, time, and place of marketing? Have lead-time requirements been realistically appraised? Have sensible analyses been made with respect to corporate resources required to launch the new item? Have return-on-investment analyses been projected; and if so, are the underlying assumptions reasonable? Has the competition been realistically evaluated?

Cash flow directions. Each profit-center plan, whether dealing with current or future periods, should project the cash flow from or to the corporation for the full forecast period. This serves two purposes: to help the corporation with its overall cash planning and to let the corporation know whether the profit center is projected to be a "contributor" or a "drainer" for the period forecast. A simple cash flow analysis is often more valuable than much more sophisticated financial data in appraising the prospects of individual profit centers.

Sales and profits; return on investment. In the well-developed plan with clear and firm objectives, projections of sales and profit values and return-on-investment indices should be a normal fallout of all other planning data, at least for the immediate and intermediate futures. If planning projections are simply statistical extrapolations of past trends or of future hopes, they should be considered suspect, indications of a lack of real visibility concerning future objectives.

Objectives at the corporate level

For the single-profit-center corporation, overall objectives and profit-center objectives are obviously the same. It does not follow from this, however, that the objectives of the multiprofit-center firm are simply a collection of individual profit-center objectives. The individual subunit and its local general management try to establish objectives that will result in a profitable and viable enterprise. To accomplish this, the subunit may require significant corporate investment. For the multiprofit-center firm, each of whose subunits has its own investment demands, this presents a problem in allocation of resources. There simply may not be enough resources available to adequately supply investment requirements of each individual subunit. This in turn presents a problem of priorities, and it is possible that the making of choices may force a reappraisal of overall corporate objectives. The final decisions made may involve such issues as a delay in planned acquisitions, a reappraisal of projected growth rates for some profit centers in order to support others, or even the sale or liquidation of a particular profit center to generate cash for the growth of others.

It is important to recognize that it is precisely in the area of resource allocation that the top corporate level demonstrates its own position with respect to the firmness or fuzziness of its objectives. Just as an individual profit center may find itself in a condition of drift, so may the top-level corporate entity. What are some of the symptoms of top-level corporate drift and indecisiveness in the area of objectives?

Overextension of resources. The corporation that tries to satisfy the resource demands of all its profit centers (regardless of how feasible these demands might seem) without a careful analysis of its capability to do so and at the same time withstand unanticipated reverses, may find itself in serious difficulty. During recent tight-money periods, a significant number of major, apparently well-based corporations found themselves in the midst of liquidity crises primarily because of a lack of discrimination and care in the allocation of corporate resources. The underlying reason for such a problem is inability or unwillingness on the part of management to make choices, that is, to carefully decide on and define objectives. Here, too, the essential issue may relate to an underlying doubt concerning which paths to choose in an era of social and economic uncertainty. As an aftermath of the liquidity crises of 1970–71, companies that were burned by the overcommitment of resources will no doubt be more careful about repeating the same mistakes.

Piecemealing of resources. Another danger that is symptomatic of top-level corporate indecisiveness is the piecemealing of resources to individual profit centers. As an illustration, let's assume that a particular profit center presents to its corporate or group management an ambitious plan for the development of a new product line. After the presentation, corporate leadership finds itself skeptical about the potential of the new line, and there is insufficient feeling of conviction to justify the commitment of significant resources to the project. The profit-center manager is deeply disappointed. If he were not convinced about the project, he would not have proposed it in the first place. To placate this valued executive, top management agrees to fund a preliminary phase of the program, postponing the difficult go, no-go decision to a later time. This bare outline of a scenario may of course have varying implications, depending on the significant details that have not been filled in. An important factor, for instance, is whether the preliminary funding will contribute toward proving the basic strength or weakness of the projected program. If this is the case, the investment might be worthwhile. On the other hand, if the piecemeal management commitment is really no more than a sop to the profit-center manager, it may prove nothing and simply result in a totally wasted investment.

Of course, if top management wants to view the preliminary investment as a "flyer," hoping that something will happen to convince it that the project has potential notwithstanding top management judgment, then O.K.—maybe. The maybe is added because it behooves the introspective management team to pause and carefully consider how many such flyers are in the works throughout the corporation. A good time to inventory the flyer situation is when the profit centers' annual plans are presented.

A proliferation of "goodwill" investments might well be indicative of an indecisive top management not sure of its own attitudes toward future objectives and, therefore, susceptible to propositions with which it does not wholeheartedly concur. The result of such a condition can be the wasteful diffusion of valuable resources, distributed in such a way as to placate various line managers but giving none of them a real chance at succeeding in their new projects.

In evaluating company plans and objectives, top management must appraise not only the firmness of profit-center projections and the convictions of line managers concerning these projections but also its own feelings about the direction or directions in which the company, as a totality, should be moving. For to offer encouragement to line managers without the firm intent of following through later with needed support is not only wasteful of resources but also destructive of morale and damaging to confidence at the profit-center level.

The time spent by top management in focusing on the careful evaluation of its planning documents is perhaps the most useful time it will spend in the course of the entire year—certainly more valuable than time spent representing the company on civic committees in order to polish up the company image (subjective, perhaps gratuitous, author's comment; take it for what it is worth).

"Real Life" in the Firm as a Test of Objectives

It was stated earlier that even the existence of a set of apparently clear objectives embodied in a carefully detailed set of plans is not an absolute indication that the company is operating with a sense of direction. The critical test of a company's attitude toward its defined objectives is the extent to which actual commitments are being made to implement them. No matter how detailed the plan, if it is not being carried out in a meaningful way with an adequate flow of resources, there is reason to doubt the firm's true commitment to its stated objectives. It is a simple enough matter to determine the extent to which objectives are being truly pursued by comparing the day-to-day activities within the firm or profit center with the course of action and the timing of events as projected in the plan.

Relationship of activities to plan

For a company that develops its own products, for instance, an excellent method of putting plans and objectives to the test of reality is to examine the pattern of research and development activity in the engineering department. Are the projects that receive most emphasis being handled in a way consistent with the enterprise's objectives as defined in planning documents? If the activity taking place in this early stage of the company's product pipeline is in fact consistent with the shape and timing of stated objectives, it is probable that the company does indeed have a sense of direction. The commitment of actual resources to engineering effort in sufficient magnitude and on a timely basis as envisaged in the plan is a major confirmation of company objectives.

Uncoordinated objectives

On the other hand, if, irrespective of the company's stated objectives, research and development activity is characterized by a series of unrelated, underfinanced projects, indications are that the management's confidence in its own stated objectives is marginal. The tendency to hedge bets leads easily to the inception of abortive, disconnected projects, none of which receives sufficient resources to lead to successful results. The condition described here is closely akin, in terms of results, to that described earlier in which an indecisive top management group provides "appeasement" capital to strong line management on the basis of unconvincing proposals for new products or product lines.

Of course, the coordinated use of resources within a single unit, such as an engineering department, is still not proof that the total company or profit center is operating toward overall common objectives. It is the coordinated use of *total* resources that constitutes the fundamental test of the firm's sense of direction. For it is not inconceivable that even in the most confused, undirected company, individual executives may be operating in a purposeful manner in pursuit of objectives that they themselves consider worthwhile. For example, a particular operating executive, in the absence of direction from above, may be perfectly clear in his own mind of what the firm's objectives should be. In pursuit of his own private vision of the future, he might gear his own area of responsibility and the resources he controls to proceed in a well-coordinated manner toward accomplishment of objectives that he considers desirable. His own segment of the total organization might be well motivated, efficient, and responsive to a talented and aggressive leader and yet, in its own "healthy" way, be marching in a direction not at all coordinated with the rest of the firm. Such a condition simply indicates that a particular manager has usurped the prerogative of a confused and indecisive top management.

To illustrate how two individually healthy organizational components within a business firm can work to the overall disadvantage of the organization, consider the following hypothetical situation:

Two dynamic management executives are operating in the framework of a particular company. One is the vice president of engineering and the other is the vice president of manufacturing. Each of these executives believes that he knows exactly the direction in which the company should be moving. The company manufactures cast iron widgets. The engineering chief is totally convinced that the widget of the future is going to be made of plastic material. Now, his fundamental charter, his prime responsibility, is to design adaptations of a basic cast iron widget. But since he is convinced that cast iron for this application is rapidly becoming obsolete, he plans in his current budget to have enough slack for research and development in the area of plastics for widgets. In addition, he has been successful in wheedling out of a reluctant management a small amount of money for some experimental plastic molding equipment. He is spending a substantial part of his own time in the search for the optimum plastic material in terms of weight, strength, durability, and acoustic characteristics, with the ultimate objective of developing the optimum widget.

The engineering vice president's colleague, the vice president of manufacturing, is also a natural leader with a well-coordinated, loyal organization. He, too, has a clear forward vision. In his mind copper widgets represent the promise of the future. Believing that the only obstacle to marketing a copper widget is the uncompetitive price, he has set aside some of his industrial engineering capability to study new manufacturing techniques and equipment, with the objective of finding a way to minimize the cost of producing a copper widget.

If this illustration were projected to its end, it could be assumed that one of these two talented executives was right in his ideas about the future of the widget and the other totally wrong; that both were right, in that either a copper widget or a plastic widget would be a substantial improvement; or that both were wrong, that, somehow, something essential had been left out of both calculations. Regardless of these speculations, one thing is clear: If and when the research and development group succeeded in its plastic widget project and developed an advanced product ready to be transferred to the production department for further action, the production group would obviously not be ready to receive it. First of all, no top-level company decision was made to pave the way for the new product; second, the manufacturing organization was developing its state of the art to a totally different end.

The ultimate result of a situation in which, within a single company, plans and programs operate in conflict because of lack of overall direction is disillusionment, waste of valuable human and material resources, and loss of valuable time during a period of dynamic change that makes no allowance for lagging technologies.

This discussion of "real life in the firm" pertains to an enterprise at the profit-center level—perhaps an operating division of a larger corporation—or a smaller homogeneous corporation. The above example of the uncoordinated use of resources deals with only two typical subgroups of such organizations. A resource-use study would actually have to follow the thread of activity through all groups in the profit center, from the purchasing department to the marketing department, always with the same question in the foreground: Are company resources being applied throughout the total organization in a coordinated manner toward the achievement of common objectives?

CONFRONTING THE PROBLEM OF DRIFT

There are no simple solutions to the difficult problems involved in the choice of and maintenance of basic company objectives. However, the first step toward such solutions is an honest recognition that the problem exists. The management group that is ready to appraise itself in terms of its real attitude toward facing the risk of change and the commitment of resources to long-term objectives is the one most likely to develop a sound approach to the task of establishing and working toward the fulfillment of realistic objectives.

Even a company whose management is truly convinced that its objectives are clear and well defined can only gain by a critical review of the current status of those objectives. There is a whole spectrum of possible conclusions that may be drawn from such a study. The results of this kind of appraisal need not be simply either of the following polar conclusions:

- "We are on course, vigorously in pursuit of well-defined objectives."
- "We are drifting; we are operating without true objectives and are dissipating our resources."

The true range of possibilities between these two extremes may perhaps be visualized in the form of a continuous spectrum with an infinite number of points signifying degrees of condition, all the way from totally satisfactory with respect to the company's sense of direction to, at the other extreme, totally disoriented. This is particularly true for the enterprise with many profit centers, each with its own objectives to fulfill. Some of these subunits may be in excellent condition with respect to both the immediate and the intermediate future. Others may have excellent visibility concerning the immediate period ahead but may be confused about what happens beyond that. Any relatively complex corporation may be faced with a whole array of conditions with respect to the status of objectives. As size and complexity decrease, the matrix defining the status of organizational objectives would, of course, be smaller in size. But the theoretical range of possibilities is almost infinite, because conditions within organizations, as well as their economic and social ambiances, are always in flux, always dynamic, never static. Hence the need for continuing organizational introspection, even if such self-appraisals provide no more than an early warning system to detect indications of drift somewhere within the organization.

In any case, when a firm has reached a point at which it is ready to investigate and then to acknowledge the true status of its objectives, a major step forward has been accomplished. Such recognition is evidence that major psychological blocks have been overcome and that management is prepared to confront the task of confirming or reestablishing its identity. This is true whether the drifting organization is a large conglomerate, a profit center within a large company, or a small, homogeneous corporation.

But let us assume that an intensive self-appraisal has in fact been conducted and that the enterprise finds itself in a condition of drift, without truly viable objectives and no immediate idea of how to establish them and in which direction to apply its resources. What then? What steps can be taken to bring the company or profit center back on course?

Optimize the Present

The first step in such a process is to optimize the present, that is, to stop the erosion of company resources that is already in process. In an economic sense, the identity of a firm is defined by the quality and skills of its personnel, by the physical facilities at their disposal, by the products or services that the enterprise provides, and by the markets that it serves. A detailed study of these identity factors is a good way to establish the optimum path to be followed in the present and in the immediate future so that realistic objectives can be worked out from the healthiest current economic base available. Even the drifting firm (perhaps especially the drifting firm) can improve its present operations while conducting the search for viable long-term objectives.

The first tangible benefit of openly acknowledging the existence of a condition of drift is that it enables management to view the organization from a new perspective. Disjointed activities, incompatible or overlapping projects, idle facilities, diverse, underfinanced programs, and a top-heavy organization can be honestly seen for what they are: the result of management indecisiveness and a lack of believable objectives with which to keep the total organization in focus. The immediate cause of the diffusion of resources may have been an inclination to hedge bets or a tendency to appease strong managers in search of funding for pet projects. But the root cause goes back to management indecision.

Honestly viewing its problems from this perspective, management can immediately begin to make decisions about how it *does not* want to spend company resources even before it knows how it *does* wish to allocate those resources. This provides the basis for a program of action, the objective of which would be the conservation of cash in order to generate the necessary resources for the pursuit of whatever future objectives are ultimately decided upon.

The initiation of a program to optimize the present will accomplish another important objective. It will give to the hitherto-drifting organization a sense of purpose and cohesion even before new objectives are established. A valuable lesson will have been learned during the reappraisal process: hesitation to establish and to implement objectives because of the fear of loss resulting from mistaken investment decisions can be as serious in the long run as the actual loss that might result, without the corresponding benefits that would have accrued if the risk decisions had turned out to be successful. Recognizing and eliminating the waste that results from indecisive management only points up the fact that the absence of decision constitutes, in effect, decision by default. One need only ponder the vast costs in human and material resources that are associated with a large organization operating without direction in order to recognize the great savings that may be derived from a serious effort to optimize the present. When this realization comes to a management group— along with the added confidence that will emerge from actual resource conservation—a significant stride has been made in creating an environment for developing objectives for the future.

Explore How the Rest of the Industry Views the Future

The problem of making decisions that involve long-term, basically irretrievable commitments of resources to an uncertain future is a significant one, but it is not unique to any one particular firm. Most profit centers operate within the confines of a broader industry. The same uncertainty that confronts the individual firm as it tries to pierce the veil of the future is faced by other firms that service the same markets. It should not be a difficult matter, once the problem has been brought into focus, to ascertain how the future of a particular market is being dealt with by competing organizations. It may be true that a particular industry as a whole is floundering; but it is also possible that some firms within that industry have developed approaches to the implementation of new objectives that are logical outgrowths of the basic capability of the industry.

Learning from the competition is a respected American tradition. If a competitor is so entirely convinced that its planning for the future is valid that the firm is ready to commit sizable resources to implement new approaches, then it should be worthwhile for an organization to make a careful study of that firm's projection of the future. Access to this kind of information varies from industry to industry and company to company. Industry-association data, trade literature, and industrywide seminars are all possible sources of such information, as is other intelligence filtering through the industry grapevine, or perhaps news items being officially released by companies moving out in new directions. Closer to home, the organization's own purchasing and marketing departments, which in any case should serve as the company's eyes and ears to the outside world in addition to their other functions, should be alerted to gather such information from sources within and peripheral to the industry.

The important thing is for the management group to open itself to awareness of its difficulties in the area of objectives. Once this is done, the logic of looking elsewhere for help becomes apparent. It becomes possible to recognize approaches to solutions that are already being tried by other organizations. In any industry where obsolescence threatens in the near or intermediate future, the likelihood is that some companies will be marking time while others operate programs to protect themselves against the impending threat. The newly aware management has the possibility of making up lost time by evaluating the various approaches being tried by competitors who have already faced up to the issue. Moreover, an evaluation of the results of those attempts in terms of actual experience, good and bad, can offer valuable insight into the problem of the searching firm in its quest for realistic objectives.

Obviously, studying the experience of others must be more than a mere mechanical process. Slavish imitation even of a successful formula is not likely to yield good results. It is only by a careful and thoughtful analysis of another's experience that the benefits of that experience can be transferred and utilized.

Probe the Intellectual Resources Within the Company

It is most probable that within the drifting firm itself serious discussions have been taking place in an informal manner among non-top management employees concerning the future prospects of the organization. Often what is not recognized by top management because of psychological or emotional factors is already well understood at lower management levels. During the period when top management has been blind to the gradual erosion of objectives, middle management people, perhaps less ego-involved but equally concerned, may have been asking, "Where is the company going?" "What should be done to get us back on course?" Such questions may also have resulted in answers that contained approaches to feasible solutions. This kind of intellectual ferment can be converted into a valuable resource when properly channeled.

There is a tendency on the part of top management groups, which operate at the apex of organizational structures, to appreciate their middle management subordinates for their technical capabilities but not to think of them as generalists able to deal conceptually with broad problems outside of their specific spheres of responsibility. The truth is that while the engineer, the accountant, the administrator, and the foreman are doing their jobs, they are also apt to be observing and drawing conclusions about more general aspects of the business, especially its future prospects, which are of vital interest to them.

Once the management team has acknowledged that it has a problem with respect to the validity and firmness of its objectives, it should take the next step and present the problem to its middle management cadres. By doing so, it will be revealing no secrets; it will be displaying a readiness to share problems the existence of which will undoubtedly be common knowledge. Willingness to share the problem will make available the valuable intellectual resources that abide among the middle management groups. Freely laying out the problem of company disorientation (whatever terminology may be used) and creating an atmosphere conducive to dialogue will bring fresh insights to bear on the need to restructure company objectives for immediate survival and future growth.

The initiation of dialogue is a commonsense, effective way of breaking out of the trap of in-group thinking and of broadening the base from which ideas may be drawn. How such a dialogue may be instituted depends upon the character of the individual organization. It may take the form of small meetings or seminars; freewheeling, brainstorming sessions; or perhaps an organized suggestion program. The aim of each method would be the same: to cull out those ideas that might be used as a basis for moving the company in valid new directions. The management group instituting such a program should not be surprised to receive in the form of proposals complete sketches of new products or product improvements; or, in the case of service organizations, innovative ideas for new, improved, or allied service packages; or, in the case of any kind of organization, revised marketing concepts and innovative marketing approaches. Once the problem is put on the table with the opportunity for an open hearing, talented middle management people, already concerned about their future and the future of their organization, may find themselves stimulated to burn some midnight oil in search of solutions that might also open the road to personal opportunity.

Review Available Economic and Social Projections

There are no prophets available to define the nature of tomorrow. Although substantial work has been done relating to long-range projections of the gross national product, these projections are essentially quantitative in nature. But the shape and the content of the GNP is of greater importance to the individual firm and industry. Lately much thoughtful study has been applied to the question of what the future will look like. There is developing a substantial body of serious literature devoted to projecting the character, as well as the magnitude, of the GNP. Some of this literature considers the added question "What *should* the shape of the future be?" It is suggested that the business organization that intends to be functioning during the next decade would be well advised to apprise itself of the projections and discussions that have been launched by the futurists in government, in think tanks, and among the ranks of business journalists and social commentators.

Although nobody has enough knowledge to project the form or the substance of consumer demand ten years from now, certain trends have already emerged in the early years of this decade that have their origins in the ferment of the turbulent 1960s. Business firms in search of new and durable objectives should take these trends into account in their planning for the future. While they offer few clear answers with respect to specific products and services that will be in demand, these trends do offer valuable clues about the characteristics that products of the future will need to have and the type of marketing approaches that are likely to be most effective in promoting those products.

Listed here are summaries and inferences concerning developing trends, which offer indications of the demands that the marketplace will be making of business in the near and the intermediate future, based on data prepared by the National Goals Research staff in July 1970: [*]

1. Faced with the increased technological complexity of consumer goods, the consumer will probably demand that advertising be more educational and informative. The product with an honest, straightforward story to tell is likely to be more appreciated than the one that is advertised by a celebrity who gives it his personal endorsement. As a consumer, the citizen of the seventies will be apt to reward and punish advertisers by giving and withholding business based on the intelligence with which he is

[*] *Toward Balanced Growth: Quantity with Quality.* Washington, D.C.: GPO.

approached. As a voter, this same citizen will be in a position to press for new standards in advertising, transmitted through publicly controlled communication facilities.

2. Many young citizens of today are making value judgments concerning the ecological characteristics of consumer products. The business that finds a way to maintain the end utility of its product while improving its ecological characteristics is likely to have an edge over competition that is not planning for this new contingency of the 1970s.

3. In addition to the increased technological complexity of many consumer products, the sheer multiplicity of new, virtually undifferentiated products on the market is causing feelings of resentment and mistrust because of the difficulty of making rational choices among them.

4. The basic quality of products, that is, how well they are designed for their end use, is likely to become more important than their glamour content as designed and advertised. (The promotion of big cars with powerful engines, for instance, is obviously in conflict with the new awareness of and concern with resource conservation and the quality of air.)

Even though these projected trends are focused on products, they apply almost equally to the service industries. And while the demands of the ultimate consumer are emphasized, the implications are equally clear for the support industries that back up the industries that service the consumer, from manufacturers of capital goods to advertising agencies to public relations firms.

Focus on Utility of End Products

The major root causes of company obsolescence are traceable to one particular type of management inflexibility. This is the tendency on the part of managements to think of their organizations in terms of the products or services that they produce and supply rather than in terms of the needs fulfilled by these products or services. There is a built-in rigidity in this kind of thinking. First, there is the basic inflexibility inherent to any physical or conceptual design. A physical product is frozen in its basic configuration. A service-type product is frozen within its conceptual framework (a given type of insurance policy, a particular kind of checking account).

This inherent limitation is less extreme in the case of most service businesses. Because they deal with "intangible" needs of the consumer, they are more attuned to thinking in those terms than in terms of service configuration. But here, too, there is a basic rigidity that comes from the power of custom and tradition. For instance, in view of the long-term trend in the loss of dollar purchasing power, insurance companies, particularly life insurance companies, should long ago have been introducing policies that take this condition into account. Actually, this change in thinking is still in the pioneer stage in the insurance industry.

The second limitation caused by thinking in terms of specific products rather than end uses is that products become obsolete at a much faster pace than do the needs they serve. Some needs, indeed, never become obsolete. For example, although the horse-drawn carriage has long been obsolete, the need for transportation is still with us.

In its fiftieth anniversary issue, *Forbes* magazine (September 15, 1967, p. 161) touches on this issue in a discussion of the decline of Baldwin Locomotive and American Locomotive, manufacturers of steam engines for the railroad industry. According to *Forbes*, "Neither would accept the fact that the steam locomotive would give way to the diesel. . . ." The magazine points out further that General Motors, a nonrailroad company, grasped the opportunity to compete against steam locomotives with diesels and ". . . through its Electro-Motive division now has 71 percent of the U.S. locomotive market." In his book *Top Management Planning* (Macmillan, 1969, p. 34), George A. Steiner provides a more specific insight into the issue of configuration versus end use, also using Baldwin as an example: "The Baldwin Locomotive Works might be a profitable company today if its mission had been changed from 'making steam locomotives to providing instant power for railroads.'"

A recent example of the need for thinking in terms of consumer needs rather than product configuration is the chaotic situation faced by manufacturers of women's clothes. During 1970 and 1971, manufacturers of dresses and skirts discerned that to stay in business they had to switch to the making of ladies' pants suits. Women in large numbers had decided not to follow the lead of the fashion designers (a new and significant development) and included in their wardrobes a high proportion of pants suits, disregarding the ongoing debate about the desired length of skirts and dresses. Women throughout the western world simply became more eclectic and independent in their tastes. (Regardless of individual views about the women's liberation movement, it will obviously have long-range economic consequences in addition to its social impact.)

The point of all this is that the individual company should not be thinking of itself as a manufacturer of specific products or services, but as a satisfier of particular needs and requirements. The major task of management in setting objectives, then, is to project the form in which the market will wish to have its needs satisfied. Of basic importance is the fact that it is the end utility of the product, not its precise configuration, that is the key to establishing forward company objectives.

CONFRONTING THE PROBLEM OF OBSOLESCENCE

There is always the possibility that a business unit's loss of clear objectives is a result of the fact that its product or product line is obsolete both in form and in content and that the company is functioning in a decaying industry. Not only is the product or product line becoming outmoded, but its basic utility, its end purpose, is disappearing. If the industry as a whole is losing its social value and the future holds no promise, this situation, too, must be recognized and dealt with. And no matter how bad a situation may be, there is usually some meaningful, "best" solution available once the magnitude of the problem is recognized. The best solution may be as drastic as simply liquidating the company and turning over the converted assets to the owners or stockholders so that they may otherwise use their remaining investment; or the alternative may be to continue operating, working the firm for whatever cash flow may still be generated for the benefit of the investors.

However, before contemplating such drastic alternatives, the troubled organization should take certain basic factors into consideration. First is the fact that the most valuable assets of a firm may be its management and its skilled personnel. The talents that successfully produced certain products are generally more versatile than the physical end results of their efforts. Business firms usually are not in the habit of capitalizing their human resources and valuing them on a balance sheet. Yet these human resources, in the form of a cohesive team, may still be of great potential value if their efforts are redirected to totally new end products. Another factor to consider is the company's material resources. Physical facilities, plant machinery and equipment, and tooling may have application to alternate uses, and the business organization that faces obsolescence should be searching for these alternates.

A company that cultivates the discipline of honest self-appraisal should have sufficient time to overcome this most stringent of all situations that could face a business firm—obsolescence both of end-product configuration and, even more serious, of basic end-product utility. For the firm that is ready to face the issue and is willing to confront the challenge of total resource redirection, a clear set of objectives will emerge. The first steps in such a process are:

1. Optimize the present.
2. Identify, classify, and evaluate available human and material resources for possible alternate applications.
3. Seek out and choose a growth product line that is compatible with the company resource structure.
4. Plan how to penetrate the selected market.

Obviously, there is no guarantee that such an attempted conversion will succeed. If the company's capabilities are so specialized that the capital required for the reconversion of plant and facilities and the necessary reorientation of skills would result in an unduly high investment, the likelihood of success would indeed be remote. Short of this extreme situation, however, the possibility of total conversion is worth considering. New companies are continually entering the economy without the head start that comes from an already functioning, cohesive management team and existing capital resources. New firms must often start simply with an idea and then gradually and painfully develop the resources to implement it. The existing firm needs only to find the right idea, the viable concept, and the suitable product line. Then the management team, which is already accustomed to working together, can begin to move in its new direction.

3

MAKING DECISIONS FOR CHANGE

In the modern business corporation, the making of decisions is a continual process at all levels of the organization. These decisions fall into two basic categories: decisions for change, which involve the commitment or reorganization of significant company resources; and operational decisions, which pertain to the normal day-to-day conduct of business. Both categories are of vital importance to the prospects of business organizations, but they are vastly different functions with separate problems and dissimilar dynamics. Chapter 5 will deal with the dynamics of the operational-decision structure. Here we shall discuss the salient aspects of decision making for change, with major emphasis on the problems faced by business managers who must commit irretrievable resources to an uncertain future.

THE TASK OF THE DECISION MAKER

The individuals who make the decisions for the modern corporation are, or should be, first of all businessmen. This means that they need to possess the kind of judgment and imagination that recognizes profit opportunities. They have to have a talent for weighing the most possible gain to be achieved from a course of action against the worst possible consequences of failure. In this sense, the role of the modern corporate manager is no different from that of the turn-of-the-century entrepreneur.

An individual may be a great organizer, a fine administrator, a gifted communicator; but if he does not have a keen instinct for recognizing opportunity, he is not likely to be an effective manager at any level. This basic fact is easily overlooked in the modern corporation. This is because corporations, like all complex organizational structures, have certain bureaucratic characteristics. They require systems, procedures, formal communication channels, defined approval levels, in-baskets, out-baskets, masses of paperwork, and many other identifying marks of bureaucratic organizations. These are characteristics which, though necessary, also have a potential of destroying the effectiveness of organizational entities designed to achieve objectives. As a result of this destructive potential, which is implicit in the formal structure of any complex firm, it is recognized that effective organization, efficient administration, and good communications are all essential to the smooth operation of such enterprises. For this reason there is sometimes a tendency to confuse ends and means in the operation of a corporate entity.

Notwithstanding the importance of these operational requirements, they are essentially the instruments, the means, that make it possible for decision makers to do their job, to accomplish corporate ends. It is important to keep this distinction in mind in the choice of personnel to fill decision-making positions. Without good decision makers as leaders, the well-run organization "runs" to little useful purpose.

The perfect business manager would be a good businessman and a good administrator. He would have the ability to recognize and exploit business opportunity and the talent to make a complex organization function in an optimum fashion. As is true of all ideal conditions, it is the rare person who has such a fortunate combination of talents. Luckily it is not necessary for a good manager to be also a good administrator so long as he recognizes this lack in himself, for he can always avail himself of such supplementary capability. It is necessary, however, for him to be a good businessman because business decisions are a fundamental managerial responsibility.

WHO ARE THE DECISION MAKERS?

It is appropriate at this point to identify more clearly who the important decision makers are in the firm. Any business leader with the authority to make choices concerning the disposition of substantial company resources and/or the power to in any way change the direction of the business entity is an important decision maker. By way of example, this might include the chief operating officer of the firm or profit center, the top marketing manager, the head of a purchasing department, a high-level production manager, a chief engineer, the controller, or any other manager who helps determine company direction or how corporate funds are to be allocated.

The top decision maker in a corporation is its chief operating executive. Since he makes many decisions personally and all operating authority is directly or indirectly delegated by him, all decisions made in the firm are ultimately his responsibility. Although corporate decisions often need to be approved by the firm's board of directors or possibly by a subcommittee of the board, this is essentially to ratify or veto decisions and to oversee the general performance of the chief operating officer. But the creative act of decision making is finally an operational responsibility.

Personnel whose function it is to provide staff assistance should normally not be part of the decision-making linkage. They may help clarify issues, define alternatives, collect data, conduct analyses, and present expert advice. However, when the influence of staff personnel on decision making becomes prevalent, it is an indication of insufficient confidence in the operational chain of command. In business, the individuals responsible for establishing objectives and given the resources to implement them should also be responsible for the decisions required to achieve those objectives. These are the corporate operators, from the chief executive down to the functional head of an operating department in the smallest profit center.

DECISION MAKING FOR CHANGE: THE ART AND THE SCIENCE

Decision making for change is the art of the business world. The tools required to help make decisions and then to implement them constitute the science. Discussion of decisions for change requires analysis of both the art and the science.

The Art of Decision Making for Change

It is clear that decisions for change that require trying to visualize the shape of the future may involve considerable risk in this watershed age. Changing international economic relationships, the reappraisal of energy requirements and resources, the inevitable future trade-offs between ecological goals and basic economic requirements, evolving life-styles with their impacts on consumer tastes and consumer demands—these are all factors in transition with few resolutions in sight, issues that will remain in flux for the foreseeable future. Yet they are factors that influence decisions in every kind of business, from what sort of insurance policy to design, what kind of movies to produce, what type of antipollution systems to implement, to what kind of fuel and power plans to institute. And every industry must attempt to project the shape of a future environment in making such major decisions as the establishment of new business lines or product lines, significant facility expansions, or investments in foreign countries.

The range of uncertainties affects virtually all manufacturing, processing, distribution, transportation, and service industries. This means that data used to project the future and the details necessary for business decisions are often conjectural. It also means that for the business manager decision making remains a risky and perhaps lonely process. Most significantly, it means that at the end of a decision-making process, judgment, intuition, imagination, knowledge, and experience must finally be applied in a highly personal way—and therein lies the art of decision making for change. For these are characteristics inherent in the individual himself; they are not subject to measurement or quantification, only to after-the-fact evaluation. Even the extent to which they can be learned is a function of an individual's basic intellectual and psychological structure. In the case of experience, for instance, it is not experience itself that is the determining factor but the manner in which the individual perceives and absorbs his experience and integrates it into his thought processes.

The Science of Decision Making for Change

Management science, on the other hand, is more tangible. It consists basically of two kinds of tools: the analytical tools available to help make decisions and the operational tools required to keep the business running smoothly. The operational tools relate to communications, organization, and administration and are discussed separately throughout this book. Here we will consider only the relationship between the decision maker and the analytical aspects of management science that are available for his use.

The major disciplines that can be drawn on by business decision makers are financial analysis, operations research, and statistical analysis. They may be used separately or in combination, depending on the nature and complexity of the decision to be made. In a later section they will be described in some detail.

Many business leaders in large companies, as well as in small ones, ignore the decision-making assistance that may be derived from the tools of management science, preferring to trust exclusively their own judgment and intuition. This attitude is based on a misconception: that somehow these analytic tools are intended to preempt the decision-making function of business managers; that a group of impersonal "experts" without final responsibility are trying, with their formulas and matrices, to tell the boss what to do. Actually the exact contrary is true. All analytic management science techniques have one thing in common. Their only purpose is to extract data from a complex environment and to organize them in such a way as to enable decision makers to apply their judgment to the available facts. It is important that this be understood, because the modern decision maker needs all the help he can get in sorting out reality.

The business manager who prefers to operate unencumbered by the assistance that management science has to offer represents one extreme. On the other extreme, and equally misled, is the manager with a tendency to rely on the techniques of quantitative analysis for the definitive answers to all his decision-making problems. The data-intoxicated manager is essentially a post-World War II phenomenon. He is an individual whose successful career has been based on an extraordinary ability to assimilate, interpret, manipulate, and utilize quantitative data. He is a fanatical devotee of management science and its tools. He does not recognize that although these tools are of immense value when used with discretion, they nevertheless have serious limitations. The problems associated with this preoccupation with "numbers" are twofold.

First of all, well-presented and well-organized masses of quantified information have a tendency to assume a life of their own, conveying an aura of independent authority and finality. Under such circumstances, it is easy to forget that no mathematical model, no cost-benefit study, no return-on-investment analysis, regardless of how technically authoritative, is any more valid than the basic assumptions that underlie the model. When overemphasis on and preoccupation with the techniques of analysis distract from a rigorous intellectual examination of basic assumptions, quantitative analysis becomes a self-defeating tool, serving to obscure reality rather than help to find it.

Second, when reliance on quantitative techniques, with or without the aid of computer technology, leads to a discounting of the experience and judgment of seasoned subordinates or colleagues, the tools of management science become counterproductive. This is unfortunate, because those individuals who for a long time have been coping with the issues and problems associated with the decision maker's area of responsibility have valuable inputs to make with respect to the decision maker's operating environment. Such individuals, though they may not be conversant with the tools of quantitative analysis, have experience and knowledge to supplement the experience and the knowledge of the decision maker himself. To dismiss such assistance out of hand in favor of programmed input and output systems of financial analysis and operations research is as self-defeating as to totally neglect the tools of management science. These analytical tools, then, must be used with care. It is generally recognized that computer outputs are no more valuable than the inputs that develop them. The same is true of the output data of all management science techniques.

There is reason to believe that the great executives of the postwar period who based their management approach on an almost religious belief in the value of quantitative analysis to the exclusion of human inputs have effectively succeeded in obsoleting themselves as a breed. This is true because the decades of the forties and fifties, during which they flourished, were radically different in their underlying conditions. Today, as social and economic variables multiply, data based on increasingly problematic assumptions become more suspect, no matter how elegant the mathematical models that derive from such assumptions. Preoccupation with technique, then, no matter how ingenious and exotic, should never divert attention from the underlying assumptions that support the analytic superstructure. Even the use of sound historical information as a data base for operations research or financial analysis needs to be viewed with caution. There are certainly occasions when past experience may be used to project future conditions. But in times of rapid change, it must be kept in mind that much of the experience of yesterday is losing relevance at an accelerating rate. This is a truth that at least some important business leaders of the fifties had to learn at great expense in the sixties.

The limitations of management science techniques are pointed out here not to minimize their importance or to denigrate their achievements. On the contrary. The purpose is to protect and to enhance their credibility when used with discretion and good business judgment. The best way to achieve this is to place the role of management tools in a realistic context. They should be viewed as valuable aids rather than as panaceas able to approximate definitive answers to problems much too complex for formula-type solutions.

A good example of a valuable management tool that has lost considerable credibility because of the extent to which it has been oversold is the company computer. The failure of computer installations to provide promised results has had the effect of developing numerous "computer haters" in the ranks of business management. In many cases, total fiascoes have resulted from the uncritical acceptance of computer systems into business organizations. As a consequence of this early overselling, the use of computer technology has been retarded in many firms that in fact require it for the genuine services it is capable of rendering.

To place in perspective the issues of management art and management science as discussed here, let it be clear that the discussion thus far has dealt with total polarities, or extremes. On the one hand, the pitfalls of management decision making based exclusively on intuitive judgments have been pointed out. On the other hand, it has been emphasized that technique alone can provide few definitive answers to the problems associated with decision making for change.

Clearly, recognition of these polarities does not solve the problems involved in the complex process of making decisions for change. The purpose of this discussion has not been to solve problems but to open up to the introspective organization an avenue for self-appraisal.

DECISION-MAKING STRESS

Another aspect of decision making for change that needs to be faced openly and frankly in the introspective organization is the inherent stress involved in the process. The making of major decisions by business managers is often a highly personal and tension-inducing experience; for such decisions may have far-reaching consequences, and they often require a choice among possibilities none of which is clear-cut and whose outcomes are not certain.

For most individuals, the making of decisions for which the choices are not easy involves paying a price in terms of psychological stress. This is true even when relatively small matters are at issue. Consider, for instance, the emotional impact involved in choosing a new car. In the long run, this is not a "make or break" type of decision for most people, but it still evokes feelings of stress. And though it is common to experience a sense of relief after the decision is made, even then there may be residual feelings of anxiety, a seeking for reassurance that the right decision has been made.

Now visualize the business manager who is faced with the task of making decisions the results of which will have an impact on the long-term future of his organization, or at least on the profitability of one or more of its fiscal years. Most of the time such an individual is operating in an environment of incomplete visibility. His decisions, by their very nature, involve elements of risk, and not until some finite future period will their impacts be discernible, perhaps quantifiable. He is probably someone subject to the same self-doubts and anxieties that affect other people. Nevertheless, he sits alone on his side of the desk, again and again required to make decisions of consequence for which he may be called to account if his judgment proves faulty.

Decisions in the complex business firm do not generally emerge full-blown from the mind of the responsible decision maker. The requirement for specific decisions might result from directives handed down from higher organization levels; they might be the result of actions initiated by peer executives. Very often the necessity for a decision by a manager is initiated by subordinates in the course of doing their jobs.

Usually, regardless of the source, it will be the subordinates who will have the task of detailing the specific proposal and presenting it to their boss for evaluation and disposition. The immediate issue might involve pricing policy for a highly competitive product or service. It might have to do with a proposal to purchase an expensive piece of new equipment. It might be concerned with an advance commitment for a significant purchase of inventory. Or it might have to do with any number of other important things that managers in any product or service industry must deal with on a regular basis.

If the issue to be decided involves a high level of risk and uncertainty, the responsible manager is apt to experience emotions of resentment toward the individuals sitting across the desk from him who are "forcing" him to make a choice. Despite the fact that making choices is an inherent part of his job, his feelings are not hard to comprehend. For in being called upon to make the decision, the manager is being put to a test. The subordinates who presented the issue to him, now having passed on the responsibility for the decision, will be keenly interested in and appraising of the choice that he makes. He may feel, too, that when they leave his office they will be evaluating his choice either individually or among themselves.

Some Decision-Making Scenarios

Different business leaders have different ways of dealing with the inherent stress involved in making difficult decisions. For that matter, any decision maker may react differently on different occasions depending on the circumstances surrounding the occasion in question.

Here are some scenarios that are indicative of something awry in the decision-making process.

The angry decision maker

One pattern of behavior often found in management offices is typified by the following situation: The manager called upon by his colleagues or subordinates to make a decision becomes unfriendly, wary, perhaps somewhat brusque and aggressive. As the presentation unfolds before him, he may even become sarcastic, ridiculing the proposal and taking advantage of any hesitation or uncertainty on the part of the proposers as an opportunity to bore in and tear the idea to shreds. Although he may not be fully aware of it, his objective is to send everybody out in a state of total disarray. Obviously, this kind of behavior is wasteful of energy and talent on both sides of the table. It is tension creating and fear producing and damaging to the morale of potentially creative and innovative fellow employees. As a result, this behavior pattern can have serious consequences for the firm; yet the probabilities are that the reason for such behavior is that the manager is trying to buy time, to postpone the need to make a decision whose ultimate effects are incalculable.

The aloof decision maker

Another possible behavior pattern may be played out as follows: The leader faced with a job of making a difficult decision listens to the proposal with an attitude of diffidence. He is impassive and possibly somewhat cold. The individuals facing him begin to feel that an invisible wall is gradually forming across the middle of the desk. He asks a few questions, almost as a matter of form, and abruptly ends the meeting, perhaps telling the participants that he will think the thing over and let them know his decision. This manager, too, despite his apparent coolness and self-possession, may be buying time with the hope of developing a private basis for a sound decision.

The quick decision manager

Still another type of decision-stress behavior is represented by the business leader prone to make on-the-spot decisions. In many ways, this manager reacts in a manner opposite to the two described above. Influenced by years of reading inspirational business literature, he is convinced that the main characteristic of a good manager is to be decisive, that is, capable of making a quick decision. His decision-making meeting may produce no tension whatever. He may listen politely, ask a few probing, insightful questions, and render a decision based on his overall impression of the information presented to him, his reputation for decisiveness intact. This manager has probably averaged out fairly well in his past decisions. Most likely his natural intelligence is high and his basic judgment is good, or he would not have achieved his position in the first place. But if his chief preoccupation is with his reputation for decisiveness, and if he tends to ignore the importance of evaluating the quality and completeness of the data placed in front of him, he faces at least one danger. The less he applies his critical faculties to the data presented to him, the sketchier and more slipshod will future data tend to become. The less demanding he is with respect to the completeness of the preparation, the less rigorous and thorough will the efforts of his subordinates tend to be. This is a self-defeating pattern that is apt to gradually lessen the quality of the total effort applied to the decision-making process.

Before going on to a fourth and somewhat different pattern of decision-making behavior, it may be appropriate to consider here the question of decisiveness versus procrastination. There is a vast difference between decisiveness and instant decision making. Decisiveness is not necessarily characterized by quick decisions, nor does the refusal to make quick decisions denote pro-crastination. A decisive business leader is one who does not delay decisions any longer than the time required to consider adequately the options available to him, taking into account constraints of time.

The habit of making quick decisions could as easily indicate a weak as a strong business leader. Unnecessary haste in arriving at a decision without considering all available data may be symptomatic of a manager yielding to internal pressure to get the task over with; or it may reflect a yielding to external pressures either from subordinates or from other sources. The business leader fearful of being thought of as indecisive may easily fall into the trap of making hasty, impulsive decisions. An easy, though not complete, remedy available to the manager who feels pressured to react quickly is to ascertain the true time requirements for the decision before acquiescing to the pressure for immediate action. This is a technique that may be used not only with subordinates and peers but also with higher management levels. In any given situation, regardless of where the decision demand comes from, the difference between a well-considered decision and a hasty one can often represent the margin between success and failure. Therefore, the request for a realistic appraisal of the time factor is always legitimate and defensible.

On the other hand, there is no escaping the fact that it is often necessary to make difficult choices quickly in the absence of adequate data. When a manager finds himself delaying an important decision beyond the time required to consider all the known options open to him based on currently available data, he should carefully examine his motives. For the obligation to choose, even in the absence of full information, is at the core of executive responsibility once the information available has been reviewed. Making difficult choices in the face of necessarily inadequate data often turns out to be the essence of the manager's job.

The arbitrary, intuitive leader

Consider now another kind of executive decision maker, one who is truly decisive but at the same time arbitrary in his decision making. This individual is confident that his intuition will guide him successfully in the future as it has in the past. Decisions come easily to him because whatever insecurities he began with in this area have long been swept aside or submerged in an impressive record of achievement based on the quality of his intuitive judgment. Probably this executive has a thinly disguised contempt for staff work, and for data except insofar as they confirm his preconceptions. It is not easy to take issue with such a person's decision-making habits. Indeed, he is the kind of man who earns admiration, whether it be grudging or enthusiastic. For one cannot help admiring the apparently totally self-confident person who is completely sure of himself in an environment characterized by uncertainty. Success needs no explanation or justification; only failure has these requirements. But this executive too, and he knows who he is, should give some serious thought to his decision-making style. Let him consider two factors: the rapidly changing world (economic, social, psychological, technical) in which he is now functioning; and the long-range impact of his style of decision-making on his organization.

No doubt, throughout the course of this executive's successful business career, he has been coping with the demands of a changing environment. Yet there is also little question that for the remainder of his career he will have to deal with changes in life-styles and in economic priorities (with their vast potential impact on capital goods and consumer goods markets); changes in employee attitudes; requirements for pollution control. These will make all the changes that he has experienced in the past seem inconsequential by comparison. No matter how vast the experience that he has gained, no matter how valid his past judgments, he, like the rest of us, must now be prepared to move into a period of great uncertainty. In the decades ahead, a good part of the solid experience of the past will become irrelevant to the future.

The only convincing explanation for excellent intuitive judgment is to define it in terms of subconscious, accumulated experience (unless one feels that his excellent intuition has a supernatural source). But to the extent that the past is becoming partially irrelevant at an accelerated rate, so must be the case for the learning experiences accumulated from the past. The successful, intuitive executive who is not prepared to recognize this situation may be relegating himself to untimely obsolescence.

The second factor for the hitherto successful but arbitrary decision maker to consider is that perhaps his success has not been as total as he believes it to have been. There are a series of questions that he might ask himself in the privacy of his office:

1. How many successful executives have I developed to continue after me as a legacy to the business?
2. How innovative and creative an organization will I leave behind?
3. How many good executives have I caused to leave the company for lack of an opportunity to feel that they were sharing in shaping the company's future?
4. Am I now the only or one of the very few driving spirits left at the organization's upper levels to keep it moving forward?
5. When I go, will the firm be left considerably weakened as a result of my decision-making style? If so, have I really fulfilled my total responsibility?
6. Have I been as good for the company as I might have been had I asked myself these questions earlier and possibly modified my management approach as a result?

Despite the existence of the strong, intuitive, phenomenally successful decision maker for whom decision making is not especially difficult, the facts remain that on all levels of management the making of important decisions is often a lonely and an agonizing experience and that many bad decisions (or lack of decisions) stem from this problem. The arbitrary procrastinator, the quiet, impassive delayer, the maker of instant decisions are each a manifestation of the fact that responsibility must come to rest at some level and this level happens to be the position that each of them holds. Once the issues for decision making are presented, whether well or poorly, all other actors leave the stage. The problem then rests with the decision maker alone, and it is at this point that the emotional and psychological stress is at its most intense. Every operating executive knows that there is an ultimate judge of his important decisions. A high-level line or staff executive has his general manager to account to; the general manager is accountable to a corporation president; the president must ultimately account to a board of directors.

RELIEVING THE PRESSURE ON THE DECISION MAKER

The decision-making process, then, often becomes a tension-filled, frustrating experience, because major decisions that have to be made relative to an uncertain future carry with them the requirement for final accountability. Yet, many executives and executive teams find the decision-making aspect of their jobs the most interesting and challenging phase of their activity.

Why, then, should the decision-making process be an ordeal in some cases and a satisfying, stimulating experience in others? Could it be a matter of personality—the difference between an introverted and an extroverted manager or between a volatile and a less temperamental executive? This kind of psychological explanation is at once too easy and too hopeless. It carries with it the connotation of inevitability. But if temperament is not the answer to why managers react differently to the pressures of decision making, what is the answer? In order to deal with this question, it is necessary to consider the manager's total decision-making environment.

The fundamental consideration in effective, rational decision making is that the emotional content of the decision-making process must be reduced to a minimum. How is this to be accomplished? The decision maker needs first of all to understand that the making of decisions in business is not an oracular or mystical process: that the full burden of making decisions should not be borne only by the decision maker, even though the final responsibility may be his alone.

Before a manager makes a major decision, he should require from those who have presented the issue for his resolution that they also bring before him all the options that are available to him in the given situation, including the potential consequences associated with each of the options. For every recommendation that involves a difficult decision, there is at least one option available, and usually more than one. The minimum option is to do nothing, to let the status quo stand. No proposal should be accepted for consideration unless its alternatives are also presented in a carefully thought-out fashion. Then decisions become a matter of weighing alternatives, of choosing among possibilities. Then, too, the individuals on the other side of the desk become active participants in the process, rather than merely salesmen for ideas or transmitters of problems for resolution. The decision maker who cultivates the discipline of forcing a joint weighing of alternatives based on the evaluation of available data has taken a significant step in eliminating the debilitating stress often involved in the decision-making process. Most significantly, he has protected himself from the pressures that force hasty, arbitrary decisions.

The question of insisting on full consideration of the issues cannot be overemphasized. Such full consideration is a precondition for effective decision making. It eliminates unnecessary emotional stress, wasteful tension, and the resulting irrational behavior that often accompanies this most important of executive duties when the path to a clear decision is not easily discernible. Aggressive or defensive behavior of a business manager during a decision-making process can often be traced to feelings of helplessness and aloneness with respect to the decision to be made. These feelings, in turn, come about because of the lack of a "handle" with which to grasp the issue. The decision maker without such a handle must often ask himself, "Where does one begin?" and "How does one decide?" The answer is to have available a set of options from which to choose, each option supported by the relevant and pertinent data. When the information is presented in this manner, the remaining requirement is the self-discipline to evaluate it objectively.

A revealing insight into the predicament of the lonely manager attempting to make a decision without a proper set of objective data is to be found in Thomas A. Harris' book on transactional analysis, *I'm O.K.—You're O.K.* (Harper & Row, 1968). Dr. Harris does not deal with the problems of business transactions per se, but the relevance of his analysis is striking.

In describing the child within each of us, Dr. Harris says,

> There are many things that can happen to us which can recreate the situation of childhood and bring on the same feelings we felt then. Frequently, we may find ourselves in situations where we are faced with impossible alternatives, where we find ourselves in a corner either actually or in the way we see it. These hook the child, as we say, and cause a replay of the original feelings

of frustration, rejection, or abandonment, and we relive a latter-day version of the small child's primary depression. Therefore, when a person is in the grip of feelings, we say his Child has taken over. When his anger dominates his reason, we say his Child is in command.

Frustration, abandonment, anger, and fear are all emotions that the manager without a handle to his problem may feel—all of them a result of a basic feeling of helplessness in the face of the decision to be made.

The Adult within us, in terms of the transactional analysis model as described by Dr. Harris, develops "thought concepts" of life based on "data gathering and data processing." Another aspect of the Adult is that it is principally concerned with transforming stimuli into pieces of information and with probability estimating.

It is obvious that in terms of the transactional analysis model, the business decision maker functions most effectively when his "Adult" is in charge. For it is this condition that enables him to deal effectively and creatively with reality. It is in this state that he is most fit to process data and to estimate probabilities.

The point of this digression into transactional analysis is this: In order to process data and estimate probabilities, there must be data available for the decision maker in a form that enables him to exercise his Adult capabilities. When a manager's behavior during decision-making sessions is similar to any of the patterns described in the above scenarios, it is probably because he does not have the information required to bring out in him his Adult capabilities, those very qualities required for effective decision making. The availability of data in manageable form, therefore, is necessary not only to make a good decision but first of all to establish for the manager the proper decision-making state of mind.

It is clear, then, that the quality of the data presented to the decision maker has an important bearing on the quality of his ultimate decision. However, there is an important corollary which, if not implemented, largely nullifies the benefits of this procedurally sound idea. Just as a responsible manager requires from his subordinates the objective presentation of data, so must he discipline himself to consider the decision-making alternatives in an objective manner. The manager who must make the final decision must also recognize his own preconceptions and prejudices and force upon himself an objective appraisal of whatever issue is being considered. If the issue evokes differences of opinion among his subordinates, he should allow a full presentation of these differences before he becomes committed to a particular viewpoint. It is to his advantage to stay above the battle until the issues are fully aired, so that he will not intimidate or demoralize one or the other side, and so that he may maintain his objectivity throughout the discussion rather than prematurely screen out pertinent data and arguments.

THE NEED FOR DECISION-MAKING ASSISTANCE

Decision making for change almost always involves an attempt to appraise the future shape of events. A particular decision may involve tomorrow or next year. But every decision is an attempt to deal successfully with complexities and uncertainties. The farther out in time that a particular decision applies, the more uncertain and less reliable are the criteria that have to be used as a basis for decision making. It is for this reason that the business manager needs all the help he can get to establish, appraise, and assign probabilities for the various possibilities that confront him.

Correspondingly, the more remote the period the decision pertains to, the more susceptible to subjective manipulation are the data used as the basis for decision making. Special care must therefore be taken to insure an objective evaluation of alternatives that pertain to the more distant time periods. For it is to be anticipated that the proposer of a particular project, no matter how honest and responsible he may be, will present his project in the most favorable light possible. The presentation may be complete. It may be based upon a comprehensive evaluation of alternatives. Yet any individual who believes in his proposal is prone to present it with a built-in favorable bias either of conscious or of subconscious origin. This is true whether the proposal emanates from internal corporate sources or from outsiders. It is especially true if it originates with the decision maker himself!

It is to deal with these basic facts that the critical faculties and the business sense of the responsible manager must come into play. He must weigh not only the alternatives presented to him but also the basic validity of the ideas being presented. He must determine whether the various options are comprehensive; whether and to what extent they have been calculated to lead him to a given set of conclusions. This is not pointed out as a criticism of the individual or group presenting the proposals. A certain amount of bias on the part of the proposer should be considered as fitting in with the normal rules of the game. It is too much to expect total objectivity from individuals who, in the final analysis, are trying to make a favorable case for a particular project.

A paradoxical and perhaps frustrating aspect of decision making in industry, or for that matter in government, is that in the evaluation of a project the individual making the decision is often at a relative disadvantage compared with those who proposed the project. It is they who have been living with and working with the idea. They are the ones familiar with its details, its strengths, and its weaknesses. (Many is the business manager who can recall occasions when he has let himself be sold a bill of goods by individuals outside or inside the firm without exposing the idea to impartial examination. If the deal turns sour, the loneliness resulting from such a decision can be excruciating for a manager who has allowed himself to be thus taken in.)

It is for all these reasons that the business decision maker should use all the available assistance to help him arrive at a major decision for change.

It is not argued here that the objective evaluation of well-presented data constitutes a guarantee of success each time a decision is to be made. If a correct approach were the only requirement for arriving at good decisions, life would be much simpler than it is and the process of successful decision making would be only a matter of following a set of preestablished rules. Clearly the complex issues that confront the modern firm make the decision-making process uncertain at best. Only the gift of prophecy can insure perfect decisions in matters that deal with

the future. Regardless of the outcome, however, the decision
maker who uses objective criteria as a basis for judgment will,
at least, be in a position to reappraise his original assumptions
against the test of reality in some future period. If the decision
turns out to be incorrect, he will be able to evaluate whether the
fault lies with the decision-making process itself or whether the
failure is a result of uncontrollable outside factors. This in itself
can be of great value in making the next set of major decisions
for change. Purely intuitive, arbitrary decisions are not susceptible to this kind of analysis, from which even failure can yield
beneficial results for the future.

AIDS TO EFFECTIVE DECISION MAKING

The search for objective criteria—conscious attempts to avoid
arbitrary, impulsive, pressured or otherwise ill-considered decisions—represents an important step in the establishment of a
rational environment for decision making for change. The introspective management team that has taken this step through a
process of organizational self-appraisal will find the necessary
tools to help establish an effective decision-making process. Here
are a few major decision-making aids that either are close at
hand or can be made readily available.

The Company Plan: A Decision-Making Framework

In the nondrifting firm, commitment by top management to
a set of plans and objectives constitutes a charter for the operating chief who submitted the plan. It also means that a number
of key decisions have probably already been made. For instance,
they might be the approval of specific, new business lines, new
product lines or products, facility expansion or consolidation, significant reorganization. The making of such decisions and the
establishment of overall decision-making guidelines in a non-
pressured planning environment obviously are conducive to
achieving more rational, better considered decisions than would
be the case if all decisions had to be made under the pressures
of time and circumstance.

Obviously, not all major decisions can be wrapped up in the neat package of a plan. Although many issues may be resolved before the fact and though basic resource commitments can be established in advance, specific decisions of a major nature can be developed only within the time and circumstance framework of required activities and events. Decisions will often need to be made in sequence with later decisions that are dependent upon the implications and results of earlier ones.

Nevertheless, well-defined plans and objectives constitute a road map and a compass for the future, providing an overall perspective against which each individual pending decision may be evaluated. In this way, a substantial amount of pressure and tension may be eliminated from the decision-making process.

However, regardless of the benefits to be derived from decision making in the framework of the preestablished plan, there is a potential danger here that needs to be identified. In an environment characterized by change, it is always possible that between the time the objectives and plans have been set and the time the decision is made, conditions might change to the extent that some or all of the basic assumptions made in the plan are invalidated. It follows from this that management must retain a flexible attitude with respect to the directions outlined in the plan. This is a joint responsibility to be shared by top management and operating management, with the initiative coming from whichever first detects a change in conditions.

Assume, for instance, that an important aspect of a profit center's objective provided for the marketing of a new product. If the profit-center chief learned that a competitor had preempted him with a better and a cheaper product, such information might call for a reevaluation of this particular objective. (This could also happen during the process of decision implementation, providing a still more severe test of management strength and resourcefulness.)

Here is another hypothetical possibility, one that would call for quick reaction from top corporate management. Assume that an unforeseen financial reverse develops in another part of the corporation with serious impacts on the total corporate cash position. Notwithstanding previous commitments, such an eventuality, too, might make it necessary to delay marketing of the new product. If so, top management would have the responsibility to act quickly and decisively to notify the profit-center leaders to place a hold on the project. In this case, the availability of a total company plan with preestablished priorities would be an aid to quick and effective decision making.

Quantitative Analysis

Earlier in this chapter, the analytical tools available as aids to decision making were enumerated: financial analysis, operations research, and statistical analysis. An attempt was made to place in perspective the potentials and limitations of these tools. There is no question, however, concerning the fact that they have immense value as decision-making aids when the correct decision is not self-evident from a quick review of available alternatives. There is also no question that the maintenance of a small staff group knowledgeable in their use is a worthwhile investment for the organization whose decisions for change involve the consideration of complex issues. It is useful to review briefly some of the techniques of these analytical tools.

Financial analysis

The basis of financial analysis is the conversion of resources of disparate kinds, such as land, labor, material, equipment, and buildings, into a single unit of measurement—money. Once this is accomplished, the techniques of financial analysis may be used to approximate the impact of any combination of these nonmonetary inputs on the objectives and the decisions of business management.

From the standpoint of major decisions for change, the most useful technique of financial analysis is return-on-investment estimating. This is so because ROI establishes the potential relationship of any given investment to the return that the investment generates in the form of profit or cash flow. This relationship is presented in the form of a ratio, namely, profit or cash flow as a percent of investment. Generally this is the most important relationship for business decision making, since the ultimate goal of any business is profit maximization. The return-on-investment indices make it possible to measure the potential earning power of investments. They are also useful in comparing the relative earning power of alternate investment opportunities when decisions have to be made among various proposed projects. The most comprehensive indices are those based upon discounted cash flow formulas, because DCF takes into consideration the time value of money in arriving at the return-on-investment index.

Operations research

Operations research has been developed as a mathematical approach to dealing with the many variables that decision makers must consider in a complex environment. *Linear programming,* one operations research tool, has the purpose of optimizing combinations. This technique may be applied, for instance, to the problem of what combination of products to bring to market or which combination of resources to apply in order to accomplish the decision maker's objective—profit maximization.

"Critical path" programming is another valuable operations research tool. It is a scheduling and/or cost-estimating technique that uses a network approach involving activities (tasks) and events (milestones) to develop work plans for complex programs. The great value of this technique is that it forces the development of a logical work plan, which must consider the interrelationships and interdependencies of the various activities and events. This approach largely precludes the possibility of missing important tasks required to accomplish the overall project. In the course of time estimating, the critical path—the longest chain of activities and events—emerges, and all other work effort may be evaluated in terms of its relationship to the critical path. The flow of required resource inputs may thus be accelerated or diminished, activity by activity, as the logic of the schedule allows or demands. Probability estimating, essentially a statistical technique, is used in conjunction with critical-path programming to arrive at the most likely times or costs associated with the program's activities.

Statistical analysis

Statistical analysis is often used in conjunction with financial analysis and operations research. It overlaps with operations research, but it has a history and a methodology of its own and deserves separate classification. A major use in industry is to establish mathematically valid trend data. Equally significant are the statistical analysis techniques for developing probability percentages based on sampling techniques.

The Special Role of the Controller

The talents and capabilities of the controller and his organization should be of great value in assisting the decision maker in his evaluation of alternate courses of action. Yet, in many business organizations the financial department is expected to perform no more than a routine accounting job. The firm that asks little more from the controller than that he keep the books and handle the taxes is underutilizing a business resource of vastly greater potential value.

Consider these facts: The controller, by the very nature of his job, is in a position to be completely objective in his attitude toward most business decisions. Except in the case of decisions that affect his own department (in which case he may not be at all objective), he has no vested interest to protect. As a result of his training and because of his function, he is profit-oriented rather than project-oriented. It is the relative profitability of a project, not the project itself, that warms or cools his heart. Further, he is likely to be basically skeptical in his reactions to new proposals. Equally important, the modern controller is at least passably familiar with financial analysis techniques such as ROI. By assuring itself of a controllership function that is modern in outlook and oriented toward financial analysis, any business organization can take a major added step in its job of minimizing the uncertainties inherent in the decision-making process. This is particularly true in individual profit centers or small corporations that cannot afford the services of even a small, specialized business-analysis staff group.

The emphasis in this chapter has been on the introduction and use of objective criteria in the making of complex business decisions. It has been pointed out that many potentially excellent decision makers are trapped into attitudes of irrationality, indecisiveness, and procrastination basically because of a lack of tools to assist them in clearly defining the major issues involved in individual decisions; that they take too much of the burden upon themselves by not insisting on a sorting out of alternatives before the issue is presented for final decision; that they do not call upon all the resources available to them before facing the decision-making task. However, technique alone is not enough to make effective decisions. Even the best documented project, complete with an exhaustive analysis of risks and alternatives, is not automatically assured of success if it is inherently a risk venture. Such ventures are dependent upon the proper falling into place of many variables, known and unknown. Probabilities may be calculated; alternatives may be weighed; risks may be measured; but these are not substitutes for decision making. They can only serve as tools and guides for the decision maker to make his task more manageable. With all of these aids, it is finally the responsible manager, supported by his experience, his judgment, his intuition, who must make the decision and accept the responsibility for its consequences.

4

IMPLEMENTING DECISIONS
FOR CHANGE

Vital as they are to the success of business organizations, even the best of decisions can be effective only in proportion to the efficiency with which they are implemented.

Even though they are closely associated and intimately dependent upon each other, decision making and decision implementation are vastly different processes. Decision making is essentially intellectual and intuitive in nature; the implementation of decisions has abstract conceptual aspects, too, in that it requires a well-designed set of management tools. But the aim of these tools is to provide a framework for a program of action: the assignment of responsibilities; the communication of instructions; the establishment and the monitoring of milestones; the detection of and quick reaction to problems—all the details that are associated with effective administration. The making of decisions is the major intellectual responsibility of management; their implementation is its major administrative responsibility. Together these two functions, when they are carried out effectively, maximize the opportunities for a successful business operation. This success formula, however, is not easily compounded.

OBSTACLES TO DECISION IMPLEMENTATION

The implementation of decisions, transforming abstractions into reality, is one of the major difficulties in the management of the complex business firm. This is true of both the major decisions for change and the decisions required to control and maintain the day-to-day operation of the firm. Here we shall focus on the most serious obstacles that block the implementation of decisions for change. In the next chapter, the general issue of management control of the decision-making process will be addressed.

The major obstacles to the implementation of decisions for change are rooted in the uncertainty and lack of clear visibility that surround a move from the known to the unknown, from the familiar to the unfamiliar. The most formidable roadblocks that might emerge to hinder effective decision implementation are the following: undetected flaws in the decision itself, poorly defined implementation plans, resistance to change, and communication problems in conveying the meaning and extent of the decision.

Flaws in the Basic Decision

The most carefully considered decision is not immune to hidden weaknesses. Just as the most carefully tested, apparently perfect metal casting may contain hidden imperfections deep beneath its outer skin, so may an apparently sound decision be flawed by some neglected condition that has significant bearing on its basic feasibility. Decisions that seem sound when considered in the abstract often fail the test of practicability because of a particular incorrect but generally accepted assumption or set of assumptions.

A case in point is illustrated in the following situation that confronted a certain business organization that we shall call Depar, Inc. This small company, whose production was totally oriented to sales to the Defense Department, was beginning to feel the impact of a reduction in the defense budget. The firm's sales backlog was approaching a dangerously low point. Management, after assessing the situation, concluded that the problem was a long-range one and that nondefense business had to be found. It was estimated that, at most, half a year was available to bring in enough new business to maintain company viability. A small marketing group was set up to find subcontract work that would fit into the company's area of capability—its technical skills and its manufacturing equipment. After about a month and a half of seeking new business, a potential customer was located: a large electronics firm was looking for a subcontractor to manufacture designated components. After a detailed cost study, Depar determined that a competitive price could be quoted for the potential business offered by the electronics company. The right skills were available and the facilities were suitable. After discussion with the prospective customer, a deal seemed close at hand, and it appeared that the company had gained at least another six months to effect a transition from defense business to commercial business. True, in order to be competitive the price quoted for the component package was very tight. On a strict bookkeeping basis, the first order would show only a breakeven situation, but at least the plant would be able to function through a difficult transition period.

However, when the plan was laid out in detail, it showed that three months would be required between the award of the contract and the first sales and that five months would pass before significant delivery schedules would be attained and cash income received. The company's controller pointed out that this would mean a significant buildup of inventories until first payments were received for shipped items. The marketing director, however, indicated that this would not be a serious problem, as progress payments against future shipments could be requested from the customer. The company president agreed that this was a reasonable solution, since this was precisely the arrangement that the firm used in its dealings with the government. And the government's progress payments against shipments were normal and routine.

When the potential customer was approached on the subject, he expressed amazement at the request. Progress payments, he pointed out, were not built into the economics of his business. He was being asked, he said, to lend his supplier money without interest, and money, as everyone surely knew, had a cost attached to it. In any case, he added, money was very tight at that time. His own interest costs were very high.

This reaction came as a considerable shock to Depar. It immediately proceeded to try to arrange bank loans but could not find acceptable terms. Business factors were approached, but the hard issue of money costs in a tight market were encountered at every turn. The price for the electronic component package was marginal. As a result, the invisible cost of money as an expense of doing business was enough to abort the potential deal. Internal resources were not available because of the difficult time the company had been having during the previous, highly competitive year in the defense business. Reluctantly the firm ended the negotiations. The search for new business continued, but valuable time had been lost and the clock was running out insofar as preparation for the future was concerned.

In concept, Depar's decision to seek commercial business was a sound one. Also, the firm had carefully matched its market search to its available skills and facilities. However, its plans foundered on this one financial issue. There was indeed a flaw in the plan, but this particular pitfall was outside the realm of the management team's significant experience. In effect, the resources of the company were not sufficient to enable implementation of the decision.

In this particular case, unavailability of resources made the decision nonviable. The issue of lead time and current asset turnover had not been considered in the choice of a potential market. With the benefit of hindsight, the management group no doubt came to the realization that they should have focused on a market where inventory turnover time was more compatible with the available resources.

The management functions of decision making and decision implementation have been separated in this discussion because, for purposes of analysis at least, they are vastly different tasks. Whether the consideration of viability belongs in one or the other category is a small point. In fact, the matter of decision viability or feasibility is the hinge that joins the two related responsibilities: The abstractly sound decision must be put to the test of feasibility before it can be effectively implemented.

Poorly Defined Implementation Plans

Even if it is assumed that a major decision is completely sound, without significant hidden flaws, it can still go awry because of poor planning for its implementation. The best decision can founder on the shoals of poor planning, insufficient attention to important details, "broad brush" consideration of potential problem areas, or inadequate delineation of responsibilities.

Here is an example of how a poorly defined implementation plan can affect a basically valid decision by inadequate attention to the impact that certain significant details have on the plan's feasibility.

An operating division of a major corporation was going through a period of substantial growth. The division had been set up some five years earlier as a single-product organization. Through astute management and aggressive marketing, it developed over a five-year period into a multiproduct division with three product lines. As a consequence of its history, the division was organized within the framework of a typical management structure for functionally organized manufacturing enterprises: a general manager, with operating heads for engineering, operations, finance, marketing, and industrial relations. The head of operations had reporting to him directors for manufacturing, plant engineering, quality control, matériel (purchasing and material control), and manufacturing engineering.

The general manager, the chief operating officer of the division, had come to the conclusion that his functional organization was becoming too unwieldy to cope with a plant characterized by three divergent product lines with several more possibly on the horizon. He believed that the operations chief was becoming so preoccupied with the daily problems involved in the making of current products that insufficient attention was being given to the future of the product lines. Indeed, there were frequent and increasing numbers of complaints to the effect that the head of operations was becoming a very difficult man to see because of his busy schedule. Problems that should have been receiving his immediate attention were being shelved or their resolutions delayed because of the press of daily business. The momentum and dynamism that had characterized the operations organization were noticeably diminishing. To a lesser extent, the same problems were becoming apparent within the marketing and engineering functions. The breadth of the product areas that had to be covered affected the ability of the management people to administer their areas in depth and with perspective. The general manager did not consider this a reflection on the ability of his operating staff. On the contrary, it was largely owing to their capability that the business was expanding and becoming diversified.

The general manager believed that he had the correct resolution for the problem. His idea was to convert the divisional structure from a functional organization to a product-line-oriented one: to project-ize the division, giving to each product line, in effect, a junior general manager who would have total profit responsibility for his product line. Each of these men would be designated vice presidents with full manufacturing, marketing, and engineering responsibilities. Of the original top-level positions, only the finance function and the industrial relations function would remain as overall responsibilities, covering the needs of the total organization. In addition, a new position, vice president for services, was to be created to handle common functions, such as purchasing, quality control, plant engineering, and tool engineering. The former chief of engineering would continue as technical adviser to the division general manager, while the former engineering organization would be split among the various product lines.

This plan in broad outline was presented by the general manager to his staff. The basic validity of the idea was accepted by most of the staff members. The engineering head objected to the fragmentation of his department, which had been built up over the lifetime of the division, and pointed out that the free interchange of research and development knowledge would thereby be inhibited. The general manager replied that it would be the engineering chief's new responsibility to coordinate research and development interchange at the top level without having to be concerned with administering a department with increasingly diverging disciplines. The engineering chief was finally convinced of the acceptability of this approach.

The controller claimed that the new structure would lead to

added overall costs as a result of functions being duplicated. The general manager agreed that this might be true to some extent, but that the cost would be small compared to the new thrust that the organization would achieve through the reorganization.

The precise setup of the new function that was to handle the common overall tasks (purchasing, quality control, plant engineering, and tool engineering) was not defined except for the fact that its leader would be designated vice president for services and that he, in this capacity, would set priorities for the allocation of effort to the various product-line organizations. There was some opposition from the newly designated product-line vice presidents to this concentration of power within the hands of a single vice president, but the opposition was muted and the issue not fully resolved.

The main objections, those of the engineering chief and the controller, had been faced and considered. The top staff, including the two who had objected, were all now in basic agreement. Remaining reservations were recognized to be minor. The general manager, enthusiastic about his plan and satisfied that the issues had been fully aired, decided to make the change effective immediately. The controller, a grumpy sort of individual anyway, complained that he needed some time to reorganize the cost-collection system, but he finally agreed that he could handle the situation on an interim basis and make his system's changes gradually.

The new product-line chiefs organized their functions and proceeded to assume their responsibilities. All this time, while the discussions were taking place and the transition was being made, the factory kept operating as usual. Materials came in the front door, were converted into products, and flowed out the back door.

Within a couple of weeks, however, frictions began to develop between the new product-line heads and the services vice president. The product-line heads complained that they were not getting sufficiently quick reaction in the resolution of quality problems and that tool engineering services and plant engineering services were not being supplied on a timely basis. In addition, they pointed out to the general manager that as long as the matériel function was not under their individual control, they could not accept total profit and loss responsibility for their areas. They argued that purchased materials were a significant part of total cost; and that the shipping of materials and its scheduling into the plant were crucial factors that were integrally related to the total individual operations, with decisive impacts on cost performance. They raised the question of how one man, the services vice president, could make intelligent decisions regarding quality problems, tooling issues, and purchasing matters for all the separate product lines, particularly since he could obviously not be an expert in all these areas.

As the weeks went on, the complaints multiplied and the friction level increased between the product-line vice presidents and the services vice president. An unspoken consensus developed among the product-line heads that they could not accept profit and loss responsibility so long as they lacked adequate control of significant resources that had a direct bearing on their performance. Man by man, each aired his own reservations to the general manager.

Since the whole idea of the organizational change was to focus more attention on the individual product lines by assigning product-line responsibility, the general manager was deeply concerned by the attitudes of his new product-line vice presidents. It seemed as though the basic intent of his decision was being jeopardized by these unforeseen developments. He had made a total commitment to the new concept and had received corporate approval for the change after a sustained selling job. Now the very men on whom he relied to implement the change and to make it successful were placing it in jeopardy. Committed as he was to the new direction, he felt he had no choice but to take action in line with the wishes of the product-line vice presidents. Instead of keeping the service function within a single central organization, he agreed to break up the matériel, quality control, and tooling groups and to place them under the respective product lines, leaving only plant engineering as a central function.

The vice president for services complained that the new system as originally planned was not being given a chance to work. The general manager agreed but expressed his feeling with some bitterness that so long as the product-line vice presidents believed that their operations were being hampered under the centralized-service concept, they would have a crutch to lean on in the event that problems arose in their areas. He pointed out that this was exactly contrary to his original intent in making the change. His aim was to fix responsibilities, not to provide a basis for having them shrugged off. "Now that I have given them what they wanted," he said, "they will have to perform."

It quickly became apparent that the move to break up the services organization presented more practical problems than had all other aspects of the reorganization. The quality-control chemical laboratory had been physically set up to service the total organization. Now some method would have to be found to split it up. The purchasing group had been organized by commodity rather than product line, each buyer being responsible for a given set of commodities and materials, regardless of product line. The tool engineering staff was geared to an overall service concept and their tool shop was centralized. The head tooling engineer complained that a breakout of the tooling shop by product line would be artificial and expensive. The chief tooling engineer, the head of purchasing, and the director of quality control, all experienced and respected middle management personnel, honestly believed that breaking up their organizations would result in needless, serious inefficiencies—but then, their viewpoints had not been solicited during any phase of the reorganization.

The general manager began to realize that his plan for reorganization had failed to take into account a number of basic factors. In the meantime, all during this period of uncertainty, materials came in the front door, were converted into products, and were shipped out the back door as usual (but not quite as efficiently as before). Problems were not being resolved in a timely manner, lines of authority were becoming blurred, and rumors about impending change swept through the offices and shops. All this time, the top management group spent hours concentrating on organizational charts, considering the pros and cons of various approaches and failing to reach agreement concerning the ultimate form of the revised organization.

The organizational problem was eventually sorted out—by a detailed analysis of how the overall division actually operated. Some of the service organizations and suborganizations remained centralized, while others were distributed among the product-line groups. The result did not make for a neat, clear-cut organizational chart, but it was at least workable.

Measured from the standpoint of cost, the damage created by the period of uncertainty was not severe, thanks basically to a high level of competence among middle management and supervisory personnel. This was indicative of the fact that a basically healthy organization will continue to operate in the short run based upon a pace and rhythm of its own, independent of top management confusion. A significant aftermath of the reorganization, however, was a residue of ill will and suspicion between the general manager and his staff, among various members of the staff, and between certain middle management and top management personnel.

This is an example of how a top-level decision, soundly considered and well based, caused unnecessary problems because of insufficient attention to essential details. In effect, the implementation plan was not sufficiently well defined. Not enough attention had been paid during the planning period to how the plant actually operated and what the impact of structural changes would be upon the smooth functioning of vital organizations.

Resistance to Change

If a particular decision, whether it involves the whole business organization or only a restricted segment, causes changes in behavior patterns, methods of operation, and forms of organization, it is liable to evoke negative reactions because of the uncertainty that accompanies change and the disaffection often caused by change.

The impact of uncertainty

There is a sense of security that comes from being able to function in accustomed ways in accordance with long-accepted procedures. Change, on the other hand, frequently requires processes of relearning, venturings into the unknown. Both of these requirements—that for relearning and that for new venturing—may inspire feelings of fear and suspicion when imposed from outside.

This is not difficult to understand. Most of us react negatively to the need for change in habitual patterns of behavior that characterize significant aspects of our personal lives. These negative feelings are magnified many times when associated with changes that have the potential of affecting job security and job opportunity. Management decisions frequently involve, on a more or less mass scale, requirements for extensive changes in organizational structure and individual behavior patterns. Such innovations can affect the positions of many people as well as have an impact on their accustomed ways of doing things. Depending on the nature and import of a particular decision, reactions to it may vary from mild irritation to severe apprehension. The worst situation is the one that leaves the individual employee uncertain about his place in the future scheme of things.

Consider the fact that business organizations develop their own rhythms and relationship patterns. These are unseen factors that operate deep within the structure of a company. Indeed, higher levels of management often operate on a plane above and beyond the reach of these unseen but significant currents, never really fully understanding them or even consciously aware that they exist. Much of the frustration and anxiety directed at management because of proposed organizational changes is the result of management's failure to understand and, hence, to take into account the true nature of its organization at this almost subconscious level. How can the elusive intangibles that may inspire fear and suspicion among trusted employees be fitted into a decision-implementation equation that is intended to move the firm in a more favorable direction? This is a question that requires an answer, since the consequences of lower-level opposition can have impacts ranging from simple delay to the actual torpedoing of sound decisions.

Hard-core opposition

Overt sabotage of management decisions by personnel in responsible positions is a rare occurrence in industry. For one thing, no management group can afford to tolerate opposition to a decision once that decision has been released for implementation. For another, the misguided individual who actively opposes the implementation of management decisions will quickly find himself isolated from his peers. Most management personnel have a strong feeling of team loyalty and a sense of personal discipline. They understand the need to work for the successful implementation of bona fide management decisions regardless of their own misgivings. Not every major decision can have unanimous approval, but its successful implementation requires unanimous effort. These are elementary rules of the game that managers live by. The individual who operated openly to thwart a company decision would, therefore, soon find himself very much alone. It is a very foolish person who would allow himself to be placed in such an exposed position.

Consequently, the individual who finds for one reason or another that he cannot live with a particular decision will normally seek more subtle methods to nullify the thrust of the decision. One possibility would be to set in motion a compensating decision, the objective of which is to circumvent the spirit of the decision without violating its letter. Here are two examples of how compensating decisions can come into play:

1. The management of a manufacturing enterprise decides to hold constant its plant engineering personnel level notwithstanding a gradually increasing production volume. The basis for the decision is that during an immediately previous period characterized by a decline in business volume, the plant engineering manager successfully argued that his operation was relatively fixed in nature and not volume-related within broad limits of plant activity. Now, management, recalling this earlier position, is taking a stand that what was true on the way down must also be true on the way up.

The plant engineer, on the other hand, believes that in this particular situation he requires more personnel to prepare the factory for its anticipated higher business volumes. He urgently requests that his superiors consider the specifics of the situation rather than base their judgment upon a previous condition. But his pleas are ineffectual. "You can't have it both ways," he is told. The decision for a plant engineering head-count freeze is reaffirmed. The plant engineer, however, is a veteran of many top management-middle management encounters. His attitude is that the job has to be done and that he must find a way to do it despite the stubbornness of top management. As an old-timer with

a strong instinct for survival, he knows that he cannot successfully defy a clear management directive. So he goes about finding
another way to resolve the situation to his satisfaction.

The instructions to him are to freeze his head count at existing levels. Nobody tells him, however, that he cannot schedule
overtime work and provide for it in his budget. He proceeds,
therefore, to budget 5 percent overtime effort for his personnel.
This is about the added labor input he believes will be required
to do the job. He regrets the fact that the 5 percent overtime
effort will carry with it a 50 percent premium overtime cost, but
he sees no alternative. The fault is not his; the added cost, to his
way of thinking, is the result of management's stubbornness.

The intent of management, of course, was to limit the ex-
penses incurred in the plant engineering department. However,
this was not how the directive was finally structured, since it
dealt with personnel levels, not cost levels. The plant engineer
abided by the letter of the directive, yet through a compensating
decision he succeeded in nullifying its intent.

2. The marketing manager of a field office in the same company has come to the conclusion that the base salary level of his
sales force is no longer in line with salary levels of competing
organizations. As a result, he forwards a recommendation to
headquarters, backed up by a detailed study, that his salesmen's
base salaries be raised. Management, fresh from its victory over
the plant engineer, turns down the request. A recent study conducted by the personnel department showed that the salaries for
the company's salesmen were well within industry averages. The
marketing manager, convinced that the corporate study is in
error, is upset because his recommendation has been turned
down. He does not trust averages and is convinced that his own
analysis is correct. Concerned about a possible gradual erosion
of his sales force through defections to competing companies, he
looks for a way to protect what he considers to be the best interests of the firm. His philosophy is that sales are the lifeblood
of a company and that it is salesmen who generate sales, not
wage and salary experts at headquarters. With this rationale to
support him, he finds a way to resolve his problem. The solution
is distasteful to him, but he feels there is no alternative. This is
his way out: he lets it be known to his sales personnel in an in-

direct but unmistakable way that his hitherto-probing analysis of expense reports and his stringent attitude toward the personal use of company cars will now become somewhat more relaxed. In effect, he has determined to add a set of unofficial (tax-free) fringe benefits to his sales force's official compensation package. This is accomplished by a simple change in attitude on his part —all for the good of the company—and he is hopeful that his small deviation will not come to anybody's attention.

Misunderstanding the Decision

In Chapter 6 it will be observed that whatever is heard or read or seen is perceived through each individual's separate consciousness, and that the inherent ambiguity of language and the emotional content of words and ideas influence the way different individuals understand things. Major decisions for change are apt to be complex in their implementation details and loaded with emotional content. It is not unusual, therefore, for significant misunderstandings and differences of interpretation to emerge even at the top levels of the organization concerning apparently clear decisions and implementation plans. Frequently, high-level executives walk out of a staff meeting firm in the belief that they understand the program for action, only to find out shortly thereafter that other individuals left the same meeting with different interpretations of what was to be done. It can easily happen that several different interpretations are carried away from such meetings. If one ponders the fact that top staff members leave such meetings with the task of activating large organizations to implement decisions arrived at in the meetings, the potential for confusion and inefficiency in implementing a plan becomes readily evident. The more layers that exist in an organizational structure, the more serious the problem can be as the instructions move downward through the various management levels.

OVERCOMING OBSTACLES TO DECISION IMPLEMENTATION

This chapter has so far described major potential difficulties which, if not anticipated, can easily hamper or render unfeasible the implementation of basically sound decisions for change. The rest of the chapter suggests approaches designed to overcome each of these potential obstacles.

Flaws in the Basic Decision

There is no way to guarantee that an apparently sound decision will not, in fact, have serious flaws capable of detection only during the decision-implementation process. No amount of preimplementation analysis and study will unearth every problem associated with a major decision for change. Certain unanticipated problems will almost surely emerge during the early implementation phases. The task of management is not only to plan well in order to minimize them but, equally important, to deal with the unexpected in a resourceful and imaginative way.

This is not to say, however, that there is not a great deal that can be done to help discover basic flaws in major decisions before the implementation phase is initiated. If the danger of a serious or fatal weakness cannot be wholly eliminated, it can at least be considerably lessened. Here are some steps that can be taken to help expose major flaws in apparently sound decisions.

Honor the dissenter

If a management group decides to make a major change affecting its enterprise, it must obviously proceed from deep conviction. If the members of the management group are not convinced before they take action, then the decision for implementation must be regarded as irresponsible. Once a decision is made, stemming from the belief that the results will be beneficial to the firm, it is natural that feelings of enthusiasm and optimism will prevail during the planning and preimplementation phases. If anything, the level of enthusiasm will tend to build during the immediate preimplementation period. The in-group (the management team), committed to the new course of action, will tend to reinforce each other in their optimistic feelings, and this optimism will breed still greater enthusiasm.

Assume now that one of the team begins to believe that certain aspects of the decision might be flawed, or that new considerations not previously brought forward are weakening his convictions about the new plan's chances for success. He may even have vaguely felt doubts all along but could not clearly define them, even to himself. Only as the plan began to unfold in more detail was he able to pinpoint his reservations with any degree of precision.

In this situation, there is apt to be a powerful impetus among the rest of the group to minimize the problems presented by the dissenter. Even worse, there may be an inclination to criticize his "lack of enthusiasm," "failure of nerve," or "indecisiveness." Such an attitude on the part of the group is not difficult to understand under the circumstances. Their thinking might run along these lines: After all, much thought, planning, research, consultation, and analysis was involved in making the original decision. The dissenter participated in this process, so why didn't he express his reservations earlier? In any case, nobody else shares his reservations. Besides, certain commitments have already been made to the new course of action; approvals were received from higher management levels; even if some small problems not previously recognized have been brought forward, they can be taken care of later. This is no time to get cold feet. A good decision has been made; the time has come to act decisively.

This reaction pattern is perhaps natural, but only in the sense that it is natural to follow the path of least resistance. To ignore dissenters or to treat them in even worse fashion is not unusual in social groups, large and small. Yet, the fact is that the constructive dissenter, with the interests of his organization at heart, may be completely right or partially right and the majority, deceived by their mutual supportiveness, may be wrong, blinded by their enthusiasm and a reluctance to reevaluate their own premises.

Even though the dissenter may be in error, the mere expression of doubt is enough reason to stop, to listen; for it is no easy thing for an individual to move out of the comfortable warmth of majority opinion into the lonely position of dissenter. The management group that has the intellectual stamina to listen to its lone dissenting peer may find that he has discovered a critical flaw in the plan at the eleventh hour.

Therefore, it is appropriate to respect and honor the dissenter rather than to squelch him. Even if he turns out to be wrong. Next time, he or another dissenter may turn out to be right.

Evaluate the "worst case"

Enthusiasm for a new plan, whether that plan involves an overall change in direction, a change in organization, or a totally new project, is an important factor in assuring its success. For maximum results, high morale is required throughout the entire organization. The initial impetus, of course, in establishing the tone that is to surround the new project must come from the leadership. However, although enthusiasm is a prerequisite for success, it also represents a possible major pitfall. The uncritical enthusiast is likely to minimize or brush aside the impact of potential problems. This basic and elementary fact represents a major challenge to business leadership groups responsible for decision making and decision implementation. On the one hand, the members of these groups must provide the thrust and momentum to make the plan a reality. On the other hand, they cannot afford at any phase of the project—conceptual, preimplementation, implementation—to lose their basic objectivity concerning the chances for ultimate success. The management group must always be ready to consider new data and to cope with new realities.

How, then, is management to maintain the fine balance between the enthusiasm needed to provide impetus to the project and the objectivity required to recognize a serious flaw in the plan—whenever that flaw may emerge?

This apparent contradiction can be resolved by the development of a "worst case" model for each new major project. Such an approach calls for early identification and isolation of those factors which, separately or in combination, are most likely to cause the project to fail if things do not progress according to plan. Once these potential problem areas are identified, the worst possible consequences of failure should be weighed and evaluated. If this approach is followed conscientiously, serious flaws in the plan for the project should become recognized at relatively early stages.

Developing a worst-case model provides the basis for avoidance or correction of serious difficulties before they take on the full dimension of dangerous realities. At worst, if the identified flaws in the plan appear insurmountable, early recognition will enable the business leaders to abort the project at the lowest possible cost. Obviously such a situation does not present a happy prospect. It must, nevertheless, be recognized that in the weighing of alternatives, the best course of action available is often one that minimizes bad impacts, rather than one that maximizes good ones.

In addition to its great value as a tool for the early identification of problems, the worst-case model offers another significant benefit that should not be overlooked. The leadership group that is conditioned to make full use of this technique maintains itself in a posture to think in terms of alternatives. On the other hand, management groups that are not conditioned to deal with "worst" contingencies are not likely to be prepared to respond flexibly and resourcefully to major unforeseen reverses. A surprise bombshell in the form of a business reverse can be demoralizing in impact to an organization not conditioned to react with resiliency when an apparently sound project suddenly begins to turn sour. One of the most serious things that is apt to happen to a leadership group in such a situation is that it will undergo a quick change in outlook—from total optimism to complete pessimism and defeatism. Few situations, however, are so bad that some best course of action is not available by way of response. Unfortunately, the leadership group that is not conditioned to deal with worst contingencies will probably not be psychologically prepared to respond flexibly and resourcefully to the challenges brought about by drastic setbacks in business.

What are some of the problems that can emerge to jeopardize the apparently well-designed plan? What are the possible signs of approaching trouble that the management group should be prepared always to recognize? The following represent a few of such possible warning signals:

Delays in the start of the project. If the decision for change involves beginning a new project, unanticipated delays may have serious consequences for successful decision implementation. This is especially true if the project requires substantial start-up costs. As the period between initial investment in personnel and facilities and projected first cash returns from the investment becomes longer because of unforeseen delays, serious strains on financial liquidity may occur. Therefore, before the decision to embark on the project is taken, various worst-case analyses should be made. For instance, data might be developed to evaluate the impact of delay by increments of time. For instance, what is the impact of a one-month delay, a two-month delay, and so on? If there are no resources available to cover the eventuality of significant delays, serious consideration should be given to the possibility that the project may collapse because of underfunding. It should be known from the outset to what extent the project can afford delay, and this should be evaluated against the probability of delay to that maximum period.

Changes in external conditions. In this dynamic and volatile economic climate, the good, soundly based decision of today may become invalid even during the period from when it is made to when it is to be implemented. Different projects depend on different factors for success. Whether these factors are within the firm's control or outside its control, they must be isolated and identified. It is never too late to abandon or modify a project if the alternative is worse; that is, if the decision to continue will have a greater negative impact than a decision to abort the project. Management should always be prepared to resist the temptation to be carried forward in implementing the project simply by the basic momentum of the project itself if the interests of the company will be better served by discontinuing the effort or by modifying it in some major fashion.

Dependency on specific individuals. Sometimes a project may be set in motion because of its espousal by a few individuals peculiarly suited to conduct the effort. It is important for the management group to evaluate the extent to which a given project is dependent on such a small group for success. An ancillary question is "How well is the rest of the organization suited to accomplish the project's requirements?" Or "Would the defection of a few individuals during the early phases doom the program or render it marginal?" These are hard, somewhat personal issues; however, they must be considered carefully. The more a project's success depends on a few selected individuals and the less it depends on objective, favorable factors, the greater the risk to the project. Regardless of the ultimate decision about whether or not to go ahead, this risk area should at least be carefully analyzed, since the performance of specific individuals can convert an abstractly sound decision to a seriously or fatally flawed one.

Poorly Defined Implementation Plans

Even if a significant decision for change is without serious flaws in its basic concept, there is still no assurance that the project will succeed. If plans to implement the project are not well defined, even the best decisions may lead to mediocre results, or even to total failure. Notwithstanding the fact that planning has been developed into an advanced state of the art in the United States, two basic requirements for effective implementation are often ignored in practice: careful detailing of the plan of action; and the use of middle management as an aid to implementation planning.

Detailing the plan

Good implementation planning of all projects, whether simple or complex, requires the projection of all activities and events that need to take place to make the project happen. "Broad brush" treatment during the planning phase is simply a manifestation of management impatience (management immaturity) or of mere laziness and incompetence. But even exquisite attention to detail is not enough to build an implementation plan for a project of any complexity. Not only does the sum total of the activities and events require consideration, but so do the interrelationships and interdependencies of these activities and events. The terms "activity" and "event" have been borrowed from the "critical path" scheduling concept. They are defined here as they relate to an implementation plan:

An "activity" is the process to be activated, the work, or tasks, that must be accomplished to achieve an objective, or milestone, whether it be interim or final in nature. An "event" is the objective, or milestone, to be achieved as a result of the activity.

The critical-path method of project planning and monitoring is extremely well suited to the implementation phase of almost any project that has some measure of complexity.

Here is the core of the approach. The sequencing of activities and events, whether parallel to each other (not interdependent) or continuous (interdependent), results in a conceptual network that in final form constitutes a network of the proposed work plan. Planning in terms of such networks forces consideration of the total logic of the implementation approach and offers strong assurance that vital details are not omitted from the planning. (For instance, a required subsequent activity cannot be plotted without first plotting all activities on which it depends.) After the network of activities and events has been defined, times can be assigned to each activity, in this way establishing and testing the project's time frame. Establishment of the time assignments leads to the automatic derivation of the "critical path," the total time required by that set of interdependent and sequential activities, which in total determine the longest time frame of any series of events and activities of the project.

Once management is satisfied that the total project network is complete, it is in a position to define clearly the responsibilities of the groups and individuals who have functions to perform (activities to do and events to complete). This can be achieved by listing all the activities that have been defined for the network under the heading of the appropriate responsible individual or organization. In this way one of the most frequent hazards to the effective implementation of a project can be avoided: having some important task inadvertently "fall through the slats" because of failure to consider a vital activity, either partially or in its entirety.

Using middle management

It is usual in large business organizations for the top members of management groups to be somewhat remote from the detailed operation of their organizations. This is an almost unavoidable condition in complex, multilayered business structures. For one thing, executives often enter firms at relatively high levels, never really having had the opportunity to learn the way the business operates from the bottom up. For another, even those top executives who have worked their way up from some lower rung of the organizational ladder have long since left behind the daily preoccupations with low-level operating details. It is the middle managers and supervisors who keep the enterprise operating on a day-to-day and week-to-week basis. It is they who best understand the operational aspects of the firm and, in addition, form the link between the organization's policy-making level and its operating level. Their range of vision concerning actual operations should be both broad and deep.

It would be ideal if all of middle management could be brought at an early stage into the decision-making process, when major changes are being contemplated. This is usually not a practical consideration. For one thing, they are too busy running the place. In addition, a large, unwieldy group is not suitable for the making of major decisions. Usually too many ambiguities and assumptions are involved in decision making; too much secrecy is required in the earliest phases; too much debate is needed before the decision can be hammered out. Top management of the firm simply cannot afford to have the operating middle managers involved in the turmoil that accompanies the decision-making process when high-level decisions are at issue.

Yet because of their broad knowledge of the operation, middle management personnel have a significant contribution to make to implementation planning for a new project. They, more than any group, can point out potential difficulties of an operational nature because of their day-to-day involvement with the realities of the system.

Therefore, the use of selected middle management personnel to critique implementation plans in their earliest phases is an effective protective measure against poor implementation planning. The management that places a very high premium on secrecy may scoff at this idea, but a management with a significant level of self-confidence will welcome the opportunity to increase the chances for success of a new project by making use of middle management resources in planning for it.

There is still another benefit to be derived from such an approach. It is middle management that will bear the brunt of making the new project work. It is the members of this group and the personnel who report to them who really constitute the implementing force within the company. By bringing middle management personnel into the project early, they are more likely to identify with it, to understand it, and to more effectively use their efforts to make the plan become a reality.

Resistance to Change

Decisions for change that require organizational realignment, alterations in operating methods and procedures, and shifting of responsibilities will almost inevitably yield as a by-product some feelings of anxiety among personnel who believe that they may be negatively affected by the planned changes. These feelings may be vague, ill defined, and possibly repressed, or they may be specific, well defined, and articulated. In essence, however, the basis of these anxieties may be expressed in these few questions: "Will I be competent to do my new job?" "Will I be able to accomplish my present job using the new methods and ideas being imposed upon me, after I have spent years in mastering the job the way it is presently constituted?" "Is there a place for me in the new setup?" "Will I gain stature or lose in the new structure?"

The impact of uncertainty

If it is agreed that these considerations are the basis for much of the resistance to change, then it should be recognized that the theme common to all these questions is that of uncertainty. It is the atmosphere of uncertainty during periods of impending change that is responsible for the rapid dissemination of rumors, sometimes quite bizarre and morale shattering, through the total organization. People are likely to anticipate the worst in times of uncertainty, and in the absence of hard, honest information, spurious information based originally on conjecture and speculation is developed and circulated as fact.

A recently observed incident illustrates the conditions that can develop during periods of change and uncertainty.

A business executive had occasion to visit a friend who was controller of a large division of a major corporation. The visit happened to coincide with a period of massive reorganization. In addition to the controller, the visitor had other friends and acquaintances among the personnel in the controller's office. When he arrived in the area of the controller's department, just outside his friend's office, the visitor was quickly surrounded by financial managers and supervisors anxious to talk about the impending reorganization. He found that some of his acquaintances were excited and apprehensive, very clearly concerned about their own future and the future of the controller's office. Speculations about the change had apparently been circulating among salaried employees in the division for several weeks. Nobody knew precisely what was to take place, but everybody knew that a major change was going to come about. The consensus among the department personnel was that a series of consolidations and combinations were to take place that, among other things, would reduce the number of accounting and financial supervisors and financial analysts. One such analyst, a woman who had been with the firm for many years, was convinced that she was about to be separated from the firm, that her job was to be eliminated. Laura's attitude was cynical and hostile. She expressed the feeling that she was going to lose her position because she was a woman doing a man's job. The rumor was strong that she was slated to go.

After the visitor succeeded in disengaging himself from the "bull pen" group, he made his way to the controller's office, curious to know what was happening. Inside the office he found his friend in a state of extreme excitement, his shirt sleeves rolled up, his collar open, and his tie askew. Scattered about the room, taped to the walls, spread across a reference table and a desk, were sheets of paper covered with penciled organizational charts.

"We are reorganizing," the controller explained, even before he said hello. Somehow this cryptic explanation of the obvious struck a common chord in both men that resulted in a burst of laughter, loud enough, apparently, to cause the controller's anxious secretary to open the door a crack to see what was happening.

When he had sufficiently recovered, the controller explained to his visitor the intricacies of what was indeed a massive reorganization of the entire division. The controller, because of his "above the battle" position, had been assigned the responsibility of coordinating the reorganization effort. He gave his friend a precise and thoughtful explanation of the changes and of their impact on the organization. The longer he spoke, the more enthusiastic he seemed. When the explanation was complete, the visitor asked, "Is this change going to put any more money in the till?" (This is a question that is reflexive among financial people.) The controller pondered a moment and replied, "Probably not." This again led to a fit of near mad laughter.

"It's really not so funny," the visitor commented, taking the liberty allowed by old friendships. "There are hundreds of people outside worried and upset, passing rumors back and forth and not paying attention to their jobs because of a reorganization that you say isn't going to make much difference. A lot of those people work for you."

"My people? They aren't even affected by the change except for a couple of promotions. Laura is being promoted to financial administrator."

"She thinks she's going to be fired because she is a woman," the visitor said.

"Why, that's ridiculous," the controller replied.

At this point, the controller, basically a very astute man, called in his secretary. "I want a meeting at two o'clock with all the financial managers and supervisors to explain the division's reorganization."

"Better late than later, to coin a new phrase," he told his friend.

What the controller recognized when he had an opportunity to think about it was that he had only to let his people know how the division reorganization affected them in order to alleviate most of the tension, fear, resentment, and speculation that was prevalent during that time and of which he was only partially aware.

In this particular situation, the controller had a rather simple and pleasant task to perform. His department was not to be affected negatively by the reorganization. There are, of course, situations when individuals and organizations are significantly affected by major changes of one kind or another, whether of a basic policy nature or involving far-reaching revisions in systems or structure. In these situations, too, the sooner that the decision can be conveyed to affected personnel, the better for the organization. Regardless of the personal consequences to individuals, knowing the facts of a situation as it affects them is far preferable, much easier to cope with, than having to function in an atmosphere of sustained uncertainty.

Even if we assume the worst possible consequences of a decision for change—loss of position—this is still true. For those who are unaffected by the change, needless anxiety and speculation can be ended. For those who are affected, notification about their change in status, whether it involves change in position or loss of job, gives them an opportunity to adjust to their new situation. There are business managers who can say without reservation that the benefits derived from giving substantial notice to responsible employees about to be terminated for reasons other than incompetence far exceed the problems associated with having "short timers" working in the plant.

Obviously, if the service of a salaried employee scheduled to be terminated can be dispensed with immediately, even if this causes some difficulty, it is best to have him leave the company as soon as possible, hopefully with adequate termination pay. However, if such an employee is required for a period of time, he should be told of his pending layoff as soon as possible even if this involves having him work after he has been notified of his termination date. Such a policy demonstrates faith in the integrity of the individual involved, and experience indicates that this will usually evoke a relatively high standard of performance. It must be recognized, of course, that time off may be requested for job interviews, preparation of resumés, and similar activities associated with the difficult task of job hunting. Nonetheless, there are substantial benefits to be derived from such an approach that overshadow the loss of time.

The most important benefit to the firm, however, does not relate so much to the employee to be terminated as it does to the personnel scheduled to remain. First of all, if employees who are to leave are notified, the remaining employees will understand that their jobs are secure, and they can settle down to work instead of being preoccupied with uncertainty concerning their own future. It should be clear that it is wiser to inform the small percentage than to have the remaining majority paralyzed into inaction because nobody knows where the axe is about to fall. Second, when the remaining employees recognize that those who are to be terminated are receiving fair and honest treatment, belief in the credibility of management is strongly enhanced. Fortunately, not every decision for change involves a reduction in work force. But even if the decision involves no more than new procedures, this can be upsetting to employees who may feel insecure about having to give up accustomed methods of operation and having to learn new ways of doing things. Popular rhetoric has it that a new learning experience is a challenge to be welcomed; the fact is, however, for many people in many instances new learning experiences, new ways of doing things, can be a source of much concern, particularly if the reason for changing is not clear and if the old ways seem to be satisfactory.

It is important, therefore, to allay feelings of hostility and insecurity that may accompany proposed new administrative approaches or new organizational structures. It is possible to accomplish this by emphasizing the similarities of the new systems to the old ones rather than simply highlighting the differences. It is easier to venture into the unknown, even in so prosaic an environment as an administrative office of a corporation, when the connection between old and new is clear and when the new can be explained as a logical extension of or a clearly required change from the old.

In summary, fear- and uncertainty-related obstacles to effective decision implementation where change is involved can usually be overcome by prompt and honest communication.

1. If the hard question of force reduction is involved, it should be faced up to immediately so that employees who are remaining on the work force can develop a positive attitude to the change, secure in the knowledge that they are to be part of the new scheme of things. In addition, the employees scheduled to leave can have sufficient time to make new arrangements.

2. The reasons for the change should be described in great detail, and the intended benefits of the change should be thoroughly explained.

3. While explaining the benefits of the new approaches, management should also identify the areas of stability, those areas not subject to change. This will give a measure of reassurance to the affected employee groups and will help them achieve perspective and understanding concerning the significance of and the need for the proposed changes.

4. The role of each affected organization or of each key individual in the new scheme of things should be clearly defined. Employees at any level who feel that they have a meaningful role in the new situation will be able to identify personally with the decision for change and work for the implementation of the new plan.

Hard-core opposition

The preceding discussion involved the obstacles to plan implementation that are a result of fear and uncertainty. The lower middle management echelons within the organization are most likely to be affected by these emotions. Job activity at this level is usually based on relatively prescribed sets of methods, procedures, and organizational relationships. When these patterns are upset, it is not surprising for the individuals whose work is closely dependent upon them to become disoriented, particularly when their familiar places in the established system might be at issue.

It is also possible, however, for opposition to change to emanate from higher echelons of management, from those who are more accustomed to thinking in terms of power, politics, and position in the firm. It was pointed out earlier that higher-level management personnel are generally too sophisticated to oppose in an open manner a major decision once it is made, regardless of personal painful consequences that arise from the decision. A controller, for instance, may find that he has lost his data-processing department to another high-level executive as a result of an organizational reshuffle, or a marketing vice president might have to relinquish the market-research function that had been part of his area of responsibility. Usually, regardless of personal view, the affected executive will accept the change with good grace. A particular controller, however, not easily able to accept his loss of control over what he considers to be an important function may suddenly find that the accounting reports coming to him from data processing are late in arriving or deteriorating in quality. Or the marketing vice president, having lost his market-research group, might establish a clandestine parallel function within his own department.

These obstacles to plan implementation, cited only by way

of example, are probably not serious in nature. It is possible, however, that certain high-level executives may be totally irreconcilable to proposed changes in the organization brought about by a particularly far-reaching decision. Their disaffection might stem from an unfavorable shift in power or position; from deep-seated policy differences; or from personality clashes that have emerged during the process of change. From the standpoint of management, there are only two acceptable courses of action for such individuals: reconciliation to the change and continued efforts to achieve the objectives of the organization; and resignation from the firm.

If management can identify disaffected employees, an honest, open approach to them is in the best interests of both the firm and the individuals in question. First of all, once such disaffected employees are identified, their cooperation can be earnestly solicited. It is fair to expect from mature adults that they will understand that things cannot always go their way. A successful team does not require uniformity of thought, but it does require loyalty in action. This kind of appeal should be given a chance to work. Sometimes the resentment is a symptom of bruised egos and injured feelings; nobody likes to lose in a struggle within a corporation any more than any other sort of conflict. If an approach based on reconciliation does not work, it should be made clear that the organization cannot tolerate sabotage of its efforts by acts of commission or omission that would tend to work against the interests of the firm as management conceives them.

If this sort of open warning is not effective, there is no alternative left to management but to terminate the relationship between the firm and the disaffected individuals, no matter how talented they may be or how loyal they may have been.

There is a tendency in many companies to try to isolate the opposition by leaving these executives some trappings of office without a meaningful function to perform. The idea apparently is that isolation will bring about a condition of such boredom or such humiliation as to lead the unfortunate person to submit his resignation by his own volition.

This is an absurd idea. In the first place, so long as he is present in the company, he can become a focus for other disaffected employees. Second, there is a strong element of cruelty inherent in this approach, and the continued presence of the executive can evoke feelings of pity for him as an underdog and hostility toward management for its treatment of him. Or worse, it can result in contempt for management for its inability to take the logical, clear step of terminating the relationship. Third, and there are many instances of this, the isolated executive may simply choose to wait out the management team that was responsible for isolating him.

If a parting of the ways finally seems inevitable, let it then take place quickly and openly. It is a much better investment to compensate an unwanted executive sufficiently to cushion his temporary dislocation while looking for a job than to pay him to occupy an office where he would serve as a symbol of past conflict.

Misunderstanding the Decision

The inherent difficulty in the communication of complex decisions is discussed in Chapter 6. Also, since communications are involved in every aspect of business activity, effective measures for counteracting communications gaps have been described in other contexts. Here are some of these measures in summary form as they affect the implementation of company plans:

1. Every aspect of the implementation plan for change should be laid out in specific detail, defining responsibilities and timetables. The more specific the presentation, the less likelihood there is of misunderstandings.

2. The plan should be conveyed through as many echelons of management as possible.

3. Personnel and organizations affected by the decision should be informed as soon as possible of their places in the scheme of things. This will minimize the fear and uncertainty that are likely to develop. It will also result in the formation of the most positive attitudes and the best morale that can reasonably be expected under the circumstances brought about by the proposed change.

5

THE DECISION MATRIX
Who Controls the Firm?

Most decisions made and implemented in the business firm are not major decisions for change. Instead, they are the decisions that are required to control and maintain day-to-day operations. None of these decisions, made and implemented by all levels of management on a daily basis, may be of great significance when reviewed in isolation. However, their total impact and the manner of their implementation determine the overall efficiency at which business units operate. It is, therefore, necessary for business managers to have an acute understanding of the condition and dynamics of the operational-decision matrix of their organizations: where the decision-making power truly rests and how much management direction is exercised.

The purpose of this chapter is to assist management in achieving such an understanding and to suggest methods of keeping the decision-making process under control. To accomplish this purpose, it is necessary to review the factors at work that tend to weaken the control that managements have over the decision-making structure of their organizations. The first is the complexity of the modern corporation. The second is the continuing struggle among management levels for control of the decision-making process. Each of these factors will be discussed in turn.

THE PARADOX OF COMPLEX ORGANIZATIONS

The division of labor that characterizes the modern complex business organization represents a method of work distribution that has proved to be highly efficient. Yet, the more complex a business firm is, the more difficult it is to manage. The greater the specialization of function, the less likely that higher levels of management understand all aspects of their own business. Since no single individual can comprehend every aspect of the complex firm, no single person is competent to make all the decisions required to keep it operating efficiently. How is this situation to be correlated with the fact that single individuals. such as company presidents or division general managers are, indeed, operationally responsible for the performance of the entities that they manage?

The answer, of course, is that the top executive has a high-level staff whom he relies on to help him cope with the diverse elements of his organization. However, what if each staff member, in turn, has under his jurisdiction a complex organization whose scope is so broad that he cannot fully comprehend all its aspects? The answer here, too, is obvious. The staff member also has a staff that has a more detailed comprehension of the total operation—and so on down the line. Each level of management, then, is dependent on a level below for a reasonable understanding of the detailed operation of some aspect of the firm's functioning.

It is suggested here that an important net result of the need for progressive downward delegation of responsibility for operating decisions (and in larger organizations for strategic decisions as well) is that high-level managers often are not aware of the manner in which operating decisions are made in their own jurisdiction, who makes these decisions, or what the basic rationale is in arriving at them.

A Challenge to Managers

For managers who doubt the validity of this proposition or who, in any case, believe it useful to check out the decision-command matrix from time to time, the following simple test is proposed:

1. Call a meeting of the heads of the various functions in the business unit.
2. Ask each one to list the most important operating decisions that have to be made on a continuing basis in the total organization (not confined to individual jurisdictions).
3. Consolidate the list and establish a skeleton matrix with the following column headings: decision description, decision authority, review authority, final review, basis for decision.

The first column would simply be a listing of the previously selected operating decisions. The second, third, and fourth columns would describe the organizational levels that, in accordance with company policy, should make the original decision, review the decision, and conduct a final review if necessary. The final column would describe the business rationale that should be used as a basis for making each individual decision.

Given a few sample items, the resulting skeleton matrix might appear somewhat as follows:

Decision Description	Decision Authority	Review Authority	Final Review	Basis for Decision
Choice of vendors for purchased items				
Changes in manufacturing processes				
Attendance at outside seminars				

The representative items shown in the matrix vary in importance. However, the decisions applicable to each of them should be based on overall company policy, which in turn should be based on good business practice in the circumstances. Some of the listed items may have significant impacts on company performance; others are less significant. Who may attend company-paid seminars may seem trivial, but whether or not there is a clear policy concerning even so small a matter is an indication of the extent of management effectiveness. For instance, if company funds are to be made available for employee attendance at outside seminars, there should be a clear understanding of what the company expects to receive for its investment. Is the purpose of sponsoring attendance at seminars to reward employees with periodic boondoggles? Is it to broaden the knowledge of selected employees about the work they do? If seminars are seriously thought of as ways to improve employee knowledge, are the attendees who represent the company expected to report on their experiences upon returning home? The thoughtful management team will have a definite point of view about this. No single decision about who may go to a seminar and what is expected from the traveler upon his return may be of great importance, but the total impact of a seminar program can have great significance. Such a program can be a total waste of time and money, or it can represent a way of bringing new ideas into the company, some of which may have far-reaching beneficial impacts.

The question of who makes decisions about changes in manufacturing processes is of great importance for a manufacturing firm. Are such decisions left exclusively to the engineer on the job? To his immediate supervisor? What are the criteria for making a change? When is an improvement worth making? Who evaluates the impact of a change on overall production schedules? These are issues that must be clearly identified and dealt with by the application of good business judgment. The author is aware of many instances where changes in manufacturing processes have had serious negative results because of lack of overview from management levels with broader overall visibility than existed at the decision-making level.

A few hours spent by an alert and introspective management team on an in-depth discussion of the decision-command matrix of the organization may well constitute the most valuable time they spend together.

The testing of a sample matrix will give a pretty clear picture of the extent to which the assembled managers understand how the daily business of the firm is actually conducted. If it is determined from this little game that the basis for decision for a substantial number of the items is not clear, then it may be inferred that a substantial part of the unit's activity is not receiving management direction and that various other persons in the firm, probably at echelons much lower down on the scale, are, for better or worse, calling the shots. If it turns out that even the responsibility for the immediate decision is not clear, then there is reason to believe that that particular area of activity is being handled in a totally autonomous manner at lower levels of the organization. Obviously, to the extent that the assembled staff personnel cannot clearly define either the responsible organizations or individuals who should be making the listed decisions or the basis on which these decisions are made, there are indications that at least for those areas of decision making, and probably many others, top management is not really in full control of the day-to-day operation of the business unit.

Suppose that the management team gives itself this decision-matrix test and finds that much of what is taking place in the daily life of the firm is happening independently of management control. What should be done?

Before answering this question, an important point should be clarified. It is not argued here that every decision in the firm must be made or even approved by top management. In a complex business organization this would be an obvious absurdity. In fact, an overconcern with detailed decisions can be as much an indication of poor management as a lack of knowledge about them. This is true because in the normal course of events, the best possible decisions will be made only by those with the most direct responsibility for decision implementation and the best understanding of the surrounding issues.

The discussion, then, has come full circle. Management has complete responsibility for directing the activities of the firm; yet it obviously should not, in the normal case, be involved in the detailed operating decisions of the firm, despite the fact that these decisions have significant cumulative impacts on the condition of the enterprise. First of all, by becoming bogged down in details, management is likely to neglect the overall management job on the policy level, possibly with serious consequences. Second, the detail-oriented top management group is likely to destroy initiative among lower-level managers and supervisors by preempting their function. Third, it is entirely possible that the background and experience of top managers do not qualify them to make many of the required daily operating decisions. Finally, the net result of such a detailed approach could be an exhausted, confused top management and a demoralized cadre of middle management and lower management personnel who have either lost or never had the opportunity to develop the capability of making decisions that rightfully should be theirs to make.

Building the Decision Matrix

How, then, is the unit to be controlled by a top management group without control of each decision made? When the fundamental role of top management is placed in perspective, the question begins to answer itself. The basic jobs of top management are to make the major decisions that establish direction and to manage the people who have been hired to implement these decisions and operate the machinery of the firm. For instance, which particular vendor is chosen as a supplier of material is a detail. A minor decision. However, the basis on which that vendor is chosen is a major decision. It may have significant implications to the competitive position of the firm. A particular make or buy decision may be trivial. The basis for that decision, though, should be consistent with an overall make or buy philosophy for the firm. When management determines the guidelines used to establish the bases for operating decisions; when it establishes levels of responsibility and approval; when it has a means of auditing operating decisions to evaluate the extent of adherence to operating-decision guidelines—then it has demonstrated its control over the process without the need to become involved in the details.

However, this desirable state of affairs cannot be wished or even decreed into being. The new company that must establish its bases for decision making, or the older company that finds its process for making operating decisions in need of review, has a significant task ahead of it. It must consider the decision-making pattern of the total operation. The many activities that require operating decisions on a regular basis must be classified into appropriate groups. The organizational level at which decisions are to be made and approved must be established. The bases and the rationale for different types of decisions have to be laid down. Methods of auditing the decision-making process need to be determined. And in the end, a decision-making matrix must evolve which is neither so cumbersome as to gear the decision-making process to a dangerously slow pace, and at the same time destroy lower management initiative, nor so loose or so vague as to take the basic control of the enterprise out of the hands of top management.

The appropriate mechanics for building or repairing a decision matrix probably differ from firm to firm, depending upon the structure of the enterprise, the resources available to it, and the pattern of working relationships that exists. In some companies this task might be parceled out by organization or function, then consolidated by a central committee, which would present the total package to top management for its approval. Other enterprises fortunate enough to have a systems analysis group might leave the basic task in the hands of such a group for the ultimate review of management—including all staff and line executives—and representatives of middle management. This approach has the advantage of not diverting operating people from their jobs until a total set of recommendations has been prepared. The disadvantage of leaving the study effort to a central staff group is that by so doing the operating heads lose the opportunity of delving, at least one time, into the real anatomy of the firm—an opportunity that would give them valuable insight into the way the enterprise operates at the working level.

Whoever does the job, however, must organize it in such a way as to allow management to review a decision matrix function by function and type of decision by type of decision, so that judgments can be made or approved concerning the basic decision-making factors. These essential factors are as follows:

1. *Basis for decision.* What should the general criteria be for making a particular type of decision? For example, how should vendors be chosen as suppliers for component parts? The general answer might be to choose the vendor who offers the lowest price from among an agreed-upon number of solicited suppliers each

of whom has a reputation for timely delivery and high-quality work.

2. *Who makes the decision?* The basis for an answer might be to determine which person is most qualified to make an intelligent choice. In the case of purchasing electrical components, the decision maker might be the purchasing agent himself.

3. *Who approves the decision?* The generalization might be that the decision should be approved by the immediate supervisor of the expert on the spot, in order to assure that the basic decision guidelines have been followed.

4. *Where should the final decision rest?* If the decision is a routine operating decision within the normal policy bounds, it might be that the first approval is sufficient. Why lengthen the decision-cycle time? If the decision required is unusual, if it involves considerable risks or the commitment of substantial resources, then more approvals may be required. The important considerations are that with each type of decision it be made clear where the final decision rests and that decision approval reside at the lowest feasible level.

Monitoring the Decision Matrix

Without an effective monitoring program, even the best-defined decision-making matrix will gradually become obsolete by being ignored in practice. This is so because any approval system involves constraints, and constraints are a nuisance. They cause delays, they require explanations, and they take time. The man on the spot, the one whose job it is to make the preliminary decision, probably feels he is best qualified to make the decision. If he is competent and confident, anxious to get the job done, he may try to shortcut the system because of the pressure involved in getting the job done. An effective monitoring system, however, is management's way of letting all affected personnel know that the making of decisions at all levels is a management concern, even if the individual decision does not receive its attention. The management group that operates a sensible decision matrix, one that combines management concern with maximum freedom of action and a minimum of approval levels for the man on the spot, need not apologize for maintaining a monitoring system.

On the other hand, the decision-making matrix that is cumbersome, slow, loaded with red tape, will eventually fall of its own weight if operating people lose patience with the system. Through compensating decisions or other stratagems, each group doing a day-to-day job will move out on its own, to the probable ultimate disadvantage of the company.

The company systems and procedures group can serve as an effective vehicle for monitoring the decision-command matrix. In many business organizations such groups are undervalued and underutilized, and they are often the first candidates for administrative force reductions during lean periods. Because their activity is frequently confined to the updating of procedures, the maintenance and revision of operating report formats, and the upgrading of administrative systems, they tend to become truly underutilized resources. This constitutes a sad waste of talent and know-how, especially since in the course of their routine duties, systems personnel generally acquire a clear and detailed understanding of how the company works, of how the various organizations and functions interrelate. They learn what the real-life relationship is between policy, procedure, and practice. And these are precisely the skills required to monitor the effectiveness of the decision-command matrix. Too often, however, their assignments stop short of this important function.

Proper use of a systems group as a monitoring organization will accomplish two basic purposes. First, it will help maintain the integrity of the decision matrix. Second, where the system is being violated, such a group will be able to analyze why the problem exists. It may be found that some aspect of the decision-making process as defined by the company is not feasible in practice. The result of such a conclusion might be to revise the policy—to make policy fit practice. Where they do not converge, they should again be brought into harmony by revising one or the other as good business sense dictates in the particular situation.

THE STRUGGLE HYPOTHESIS

The second factor that tends to erode management control of the decision-making process is the existence, at all operating levels of the modern corporation, of capable, resourceful people who believe they know better than anyone else what is best for the company—at least with respect to their own areas of responsibility. The negative result of this essentially positive and constructive condition is that a continuing struggle takes place among the various management levels for control of the decision-making process in the firm.

It is true from a theoretical standpoint that upper management has the power to make its will prevail, but this is only the case if it can ascertain when and where its will is being thwarted. Often, because of the complexity of business organizations, higher management does not have the downward visibility, hence the knowledge, to make its wishes prevail throughout the company.

As opposed to the power of top management, the lower levels of management have the advantage of a more detailed knowledge of the operation of the firm. It is precisely this balance of power in modern business organizations that provides the dynamics for the continuing struggle between management echelons for control of the decision-making process. Each time a division general manager tries to change a decision of his boss (group executive or company president), this struggle is being waged. When the chief of an engineering laboratory conducts a bootleg project that his management did not or would not approve, he too is fighting for control of the decision-making process. When a plant engineer, refused permission to hire more personnel, increases his use of overtime labor to circumvent the policy, he is wresting control of the decision-making process from higher levels of management. These compensating decisions are symptoms of this continuing struggle for control.

Submerging the Problem

It is, then, a basic aspect of life in the business world that the struggle for control does take place and that the condition permeates all management levels. Now the question arises as to why such a fundamental issue is not openly addressed by management circles. Usually, when the issue is recognized at all, it is at some visceral level by means of an irritable reaction. Which subordinate has not heard comments such as these from a boss or supervisor: "Why can't I ever get things done around this plant?" "I thought we put that plan into effect six months ago." "Whoever made that jackass decision?" "Everybody but me knows what's going on around here."

Indeed, a classic comment of this nature was attributed to President Truman. He is paraphrased as having commented about his relationship to the federal bureaucracy, "I push a button—and nothing happens."

The problem exists in business as well. Why is it not more openly addressed in business circles? Perhaps because the idea of a business organization operating in a condition of permanent struggle somehow runs against the grain. As is the case with society as a whole, the business community is to a considerable extent a servant of its own myths and its own clichés. How can a business enterprise openly accept the idea that it is an organization at war with itself, when the ideal business organization is described as a smoothly functioning team whose chief characteristics are teamwork, harmony, loyalty, and efficiency? In the face of such illusions, to admit that some kind of internal struggle is taking place in the company would appear equivalent to a confession of failure. And what chief executive would be willing even to hint at the possibility of being a failure at his job, even to himself? It is much easier to bury the problem and perpetuate the myth.

On the other hand, consider the situation of subordinate executives, managers, and supervisors. How are they to recognize the problem? Are they to say, "Look, boss, you and I are operating in a state of constant struggle. You want things your way, yet I know better than you how to operate my own part of this organization."

The conventional wisdom of how to deal with the boss suggests exactly the opposite. The prevailing idea is that if a subordinate has a project he wants to put across, the thing to do is make the boss think the idea is his. In other words, the last thing in the world to discuss openly is that there is indeed a struggle for control of the decision-making process. This piece of conventional wisdom, to make the boss think the idea is his, is in itself a tacit admission of the existence of the struggle.

Surfacing the Problem

Although it may be unpleasant or distasteful for higher management to acknowledge that the problem is a real one, it is very important that the issue be confronted. The perceptive leadership group will not hesitate to test the "struggle hypothesis." If it turns out that the organization is operating smoothly and harmoniously, totally in accord, then nothing will have been lost. On the other hand, if investigation reveals evidence of a widespread prevalence at lower levels of compensating decisions, bootleg operations, and significant foot-dragging in complying with management directives, indications are that the organization's decision-command matrix is in trouble and that intensive efforts are required to correct the situation.

The introspective management group will not approach this task in a spirit of vindictiveness. They will first of all look inward. They will want to know what it is about their management methods that has caused subordinate echelons to resort to countervailing techniques designed to thwart the intentions of higher management. Why have responsible subordinate managers found it appropriate to set in motion compensating decisions? Why have bootleg projects been established? Why have management directives been shunted aside or implemented only halfheartedly?

The answers to such questions will provide insights that will enable the introspective management group to understand the nature and the dynamics of the organization, perhaps for the first time. For as serious as they may seem, these conditions are no more than symptoms of even greater problems, probably originating within the ranks of the higher management group itself.

It is always possible, of course, that the kind of subversion represented by compensating decisions, bootleg projects, and lower-echelon foot-dragging is the work of malcontents and innately disloyal or lazy subordinates. However, to act on this assumption is at once too easy and too dangerous. It is far more likely that the problem is fundamental in nature; and if this is indeed the case, disciplinary action is the wrong cure. It will only mask the problem, not solve it.

To deal with the problem of organizational insubordination, it is necessary to bring into focus the kind of environment in which compensating decisions, bootleg projects, and subordinate foot-dragging are likely to develop and spread. A discussion of each of these techniques follows.

Compensating decisions

Let us return to one of the examples of compensating decisions that was described earlier: the case of the plant engineer who thinks he needs more personnel.

You will recall that in our example management decided to hold the plant engineering force constant, despite an increase in plant activity, because during a previous downturn the plant engineer had insisted that his work requirements were relatively fixed and, therefore, that he could not diminish his work force. Then, when business was increasing, he requested added personnel. Management refused his request based on the simple but plausible grounds that "what was true on the way down must also be true on the way up."

Plausible as this management decision might have been, it could, nevertheless, have been wrong for the following reasons:

1. During the earlier period, the plant engineer might have overstated his case and gotten away with it. If so, boxing him in with his own decision might constitute a form of poetic justice. But satisfying as this might be, it does not serve the interests of the firm if more personnel are indeed required to cope with expanded activity.

2. As a generalization, it might be true that the plant engineering force should be relatively fixed: that the plant engineer's earlier claim and the subsequent management conclusion were both right. However, the circumstances surrounding the particular business expansion might have indeed called for extra plant engineering effort because of unusual plant rearrangement, more than usual machinery maintenance, or any number of other unusual requirements.

3. The plant engineer might indeed be overestimating his requirements to cope with the business expansion.

The issue, however, is not which of these hypotheses is correct but how management arrived at its conclusion to keep the plant engineering force constant. Notwithstanding the fact that its decision was based on appraisal of an earlier situation, the final decision was basically arbitrary. It was not predicated upon the facts involved in the current situation; the past was simply projected into the future. In addition, there would be reason to suspect that a certain amount of vindictiveness had entered into the decision-making process.

In summary, a compensating decision is the response of a manager to directives or decisions from higher management that he deems unfeasible or arbitrary. The manager who feels boxed in by a higher-level decision and inhibited from getting his job done will do his best with the resources that he commands to find a way to circumvent the decision. If such compensating decisions are found to be commonly resorted to in the organization, higher-level management may well ask, "Are our directives arbitrary, insufficiently thought out, willful, whimsical, or vindictive?" "Are we failing to have enough dialogue with our subordinates before issuing operating directives?"

Bootleg projects

Why bootleg projects? This issue was discussed in some detail in Chapter 2. Here we will bring it into clearer focus as it applies to the struggle hypothesis.

In the earlier discussion, it was pointed out that when top management is confused about its objectives, other management levels are likely to move in and fill the vacuum. This will happen when strong and imaginative operating managers, lacking direction from above, have powerful convictions of their own in the area of business objectives. In this instance, the message to higher levels is clear: a first priority is to bring the organization back on course.

However, it is possible to have bootleg projects in a firm even when the company does have clear objectives. They then take place for one of two basic reasons: either higher management has failed to communicate its own enthusiasm and a sense of conviction about its objectives; or certain operating managers are so enamored of their own pet ideas that they will try to find a way to implement them, regardless of the firm's overall objectives.

The first condition is more manageable than the second. Perhaps the top management team has simply been taking too much for granted the agreement and concurrence of other management levels. It is not difficult for a dedicated and enthusiastic management group to assume that its own firmly held convictions and enthusiasms are shared by others. But this does not have to be the case. It is an integral part of management's task in the complex firm *actively* to communicate and disseminate its own beliefs throughout the organization. This is the essence of good business communications. Merely to direct and instruct is not a sufficient exercise of leadership in a business firm operating in a free society, where managers are accustomed to thinking for themselves. As will be pointed out in the next chapter, business communications must be far more than the clear dissemination of instructions, though, obviously, this is of vital importance.

The manager who is determined to have his way, regardless of the clarity of top management objectives and the intensive efforts of higher management to explain and convince, presents a more difficult problem, perhaps an unsolvable one.

There are individuals who are simply incapable of being team players in a business environment. If the top management team has honestly appraised itself, believes that it has indeed established valid and achievable objectives, and has attempted to convey its belief, then the initiator of a bootleg project presents a real disciplinary problem. If he cannot be made to understand the importance of mutual loyalty and teamwork in a business firm, then a parting of the ways is in order. This is true regardless of the capability and talent of the manager in question. If he will not recognize his responsibility as a member of the management cadre, he probably belongs in business for himself where his will can always prevail.

In the more likely situation, however, the bootleg project is a lower management reaction to lack of direction from above. It is an attempt to fill a vacuum in the area of coordinated goals and objectives. Either higher management lacks the conviction necessary to channel its resources in pursuit of coordinated objectives or, if such convictions exist, it has failed to communicate them effectively. Therefore, the lower-level manager feels free to use whatever resources he has available in pursuit of objectives *he* deems valid.

Foot-dragging

Failure to respond or a slow reaction to directives or requests is another means of blunting the effectiveness of higher management. This kind of foot-dragging may, of course, be totally innocent or inadvertent. Slowness of reaction could be caused by workload problems; failure to comply at all might be a result of simple forgetfulness.

However, lack of responsiveness can also be a calculated method of avoiding management direction. In this case, foot-dragging is simply an added weapon in the interechelon struggle among management groups for control of the decision-making process in the firm. As opposed to compensating decisions and bootleg operations, which are active, aggressive techniques, lack of responsiveness, or foot-dragging, is a form of passive resistance. It is also more difficult to detect as a countermanagement technique. When confronted with the failure to carry out a management instruction, one can always claim the press of other work. For this reason, foot-dragging is usually confined to projects not associated with a specific time constraint.

Deliberate lack of responsiveness may have various causes. The particular management directive or request may be considered an unnecessary nuisance; or the individual charged with fulfilling the directive may simply disagree with it; or he may believe that it has threatening implications.

The unnecessary nuisance might be a request for a new report. Management might want to be given data that it had not had access to before. Or perhaps a new report format involving added work might be asked for. This sort of situation is relatively trivial in impact.

There are occasions, however, when management directives of greater substance somehow run against the grain of subordinate management levels with implementing responsibilities. Often such issues, though of real substance, may be given relatively low priority ratings based on the excuse of more pressing, immediate business.

Here are examples of perfectly valid higher management directives that might lead to lower-echelon resistance:

1. The institution of a formal preventative maintenance program where none has been in effect (a plant engineering responsibility).
2. The establishment of a formal personnel evaluation plan to determine overall human resource capability (an industrial relations responsibility).
3. A manufacturing company with a substantial metal fabrication capability wants to investigate buying more parts and components and making less in house (an operational or manufacturing engineering responsibility).

The first two directives might be coolly received by the responsible functions because the projects involved were construed as implying criticisms of past performance or because they were deemed to be unnecessary additions to already heavy workloads.

The proposal in the third example might evoke more deep-seated opposition. The functional leader to whom such a proposal was addressed might view its implementation as a danger to the basic manufacturing capacity of his organization, a capability that he may have worked long and hard to develop.

Whatever the particular project may be, the delaying tactics applied by lower management levels will come into play as a result of the belief that such tactics are the only available recourse, that higher management for one reason or another will not be susceptible to arguments to suspend the projects in question; or because delaying tactics have proved effective before and represent the path of least resistance.

In general, the widespread use of foot-dragging techniques gives an important indication of the view held by lower management personnel about their superiors. Such tactics are essentially tests of management memory, conviction, and follow-through ability. There is, therefore, a certain logic attached to foot-dragging when it applies to a particular project. If nothing else, it will test management seriousness about and dedication to the proposal. If the proposal has been assigned a low priority level, there is at least a chance that management will not follow through and will let the project die. So from the viewpoint of the subordinate manager who opposes the directive, delaying tactics may seem a valid and fair way of separating management whim from management conviction.

Dealing with the Problem

The purpose in testing the struggle hypothesis is to give higher levels of management an insight into the extent to which they truly control the decision-making process in the firm. It is the effectiveness of upper management that is primarily at issue, not loyalty or probity among the lower management groups. It is important, therefore, that such an investigation have none of the characteristics of a witch-hunt. An astute management group, sensitive to the possible existence of compensating decisions, bootleg projects, and lower-level delay tactics, will be able to detect the symptoms of these techniques largely by observation alone.

In the case of delaying tactics, the affected manager need only review his follow-up file (if he has one), or ransack his memory (if he has no file), and list the projects that should be in process or completed. If the list is large and old and shows little or no activity in the items, indications are that his administrative effectiveness is questionable.

Bootleg operations of any size can be detected relatively easily within a single installation by a controller-office study of labor charges. When a division head is conducting bootleg projects that are large enough to have required higher-level approval, only a strong link between the division controller's organization and the corporate or group controller is likely to surface the issue. However, recourse to this kind of organized study should be used only as a last resort and in organizations where the decision-command structure has already proved to be ineffective and immediate, drastic action is required.

Compensating decisions represent a more difficult problem in detection. They are possible basically because every system has loopholes. The likelihood of compensating decisions can best be minimized by policies and procedures and budgeting methods that are designed in such a way as to insure management attention to significant items. For instance, a compensating decision to add overtime work in lieu of people is difficult to institute in an organization where budgets are analyzed on the basis of monetary values as well as physical head counts.

What if a management group makes a study of the decision-command matrix and finds significant evidence of compensating decisions, bootleg projects, and slow reaction to management directives? What kind of management response is appropriate in such a situation?

The most important first principle underlying a study of the decision-command matrix is to establish early the spirit of the inquiry. It should be made clear at the outset that at issue is a review of higher management effectiveness and control, not a search for disloyal subordinates. It follows from this that not even a hint of vindictiveness should be evident. This is true for several basic reasons: If higher management has been faring poorly in the interechelon power struggle, it is essentially a reflection on higher management, not on the subordinate echelons. It is management techniques that are under review, not subordinate management personnel. Also, the worst "offenders" will probably be found among the most vital, talented, and resourceful members of the organization. It takes courage, imagination, and resourcefulness—all skills of the strong manager—to set in motion bootleg projects and compensating decisions. Despite the difficulty of accepting this idea, higher management should consider the players of these "games" as valuable company resources to be handled with care. In the complex, multilayered organization, the terms "higher" and "lower" management are relative. It is completely possible for a division executive to set in motion a compensating decision or to implement a bootleg project aimed at circumventing a higher-level decision while at the same time his own subordinates are giving him the same treatment—and so on up and down the line. Therefore, before waxing indignant over subordinate disloyalty, let the manager probe his own present and past performance in this area.

The example of the permissive parent suddenly turned authoritarian is pertinent to the manager or management group newly determined to more strictly exercise its authority. The parents who, either by philosophy or neglect, have dealt with their children on a laissez-faire basis, allowing them great freedom from control from an early age, have in effect created a specific pattern of relationships between themselves and their children. The children, consequently, have a right to continue behaving in a way that has been either encouraged or condoned by their parents over a period of time. Suddenly to change this relationship, to demand strict obedience where little was required before, can only foster confusion and resentment in the youngsters. If, during all the yesterdays, a particular pattern of behavior was tolerated, why the sudden change without warning today?

The writer has no advice to offer the parents who change their child-rearing philosophy except to point out that any solution should consider that the problem was of *their* making, not of their children's. But the analogy to a management suddenly aware that it needs to strengthen its control of the decision matrix is clear. For a higher-level manager to recriminate his subordinates concerning long-established practices that have been condoned or overlooked in the past is to spring an unfair surprise. Feelings of resentment and a sense of injustice are not unreasonable under the circumstances.

Yet it is true that the prevalence of bootleg practices, compensating decisions, and lower management delaying tactics has to be kept to a minimum in the firm. This is the case, not because of abstract disciplinary reasons, but because such conditions tend to erode management effectiveness and to dissipate and fragment corporate resources.

What, then, is an appropriate management response to the discovery of lower-level resistance tactics?

1. Management should accept full responsibility for their existence.

2. It must make clear that management intends to exercise greater control than heretofore.

3. Bootleg operations or compensating decisions that have surfaced should be evaluated on an objective basis from the standpoint of their impact on the firm. Determination should be made to continue or discontinue them for reasons other than that they originated without approval. Where projects are discontinued, the reasons should be carefully explained.

4. Projects that have been assigned and then neglected should be reevaluated in the light of current thinking. If they are still considered important, they should be reassigned with

specific deadlines—and clear notice that management will follow through on their status. It should also be emphasized that forthright discussions should be held when lower echelons question the value of a project, that management is not only receptive to but needs honest feedback concerning the validity of directed or suggested projects.

5. Once these clear rules of the game are established, it should be reemphasized that they are prospective and that the game begins from then on—with one team and one set of rules.

Still, after arriving at this set of realizations and taking appropriate actions, management must recognize that the end of the story has not really been reached. The struggle will continue for control of the management process. People will still try to do things their own way. Higher managers, no matter how perceptive, will not be perfect. Lower managers, no matter how loyal, will still be independent, perhaps willful.

THE ISSUE IN PERSPECTIVE

Before concluding this discussion of the decision-command matrix, it is worth pondering together the fundamental reasons why the issue of management control of the decision-making process is far more than merely a problem in corporate discipline.

A good manager or supervisor working in a modern industrial firm is likely to develop a proprietary attitude toward the limited section of the enterprise that he controls. This is often how it is and this is how it should be. If the large, impersonal business corporation did not in reality consist of many small personal worlds, it would fall of its own weight. This is because shareholders who "own" the corporation are usually remote from its direct management and it is the employees and not the owners who control the destiny of the corporate firm.

The obvious rewards to management employees are the salaries, bonuses, and fringe benefits they receive. But it would be a serious error to believe that these economic interests are sufficient to explain the devotion, emotional involvement, and sense of responsibility that they bring to their jobs. The more abiding, if less apparent, explanation is that business leaders at all levels, from corporation president to shop foreman, spend the best part of their waking hours, year after year, on their jobs. It is on the job that they have the best opportunity to utilize their talents and to accept challenges to their ingenuity. It may be fun to watch television or play golf. These are activities to divert the tired man—or the boy within the man—but it is on the job that he earns his self-esteem, as well as his pay.

The emotional involvement that business managers and supervisors have with their jobs is, then, the basis on which the complex, modern corporation stands. This same involvement, however, presents one of the great challenges with which top management must contend. The theme of this chapter has been "Who really controls the firm?" It has been suggested that there is a continuing struggle among all levels of management for control. It is clear that top management must control the organization for which it is responsible. However, there are devoted management personnel on other levels who think that they know what is best, at least in their little corner of the company. Left to himself, the talented, interested manager will try to do things his own way and to make decisions (perhaps compensating decisions) to the best of his understanding. This would probably work out fine in most cases, if all the little worlds within the corporation were really separate ones, unrelated and not mutually dependent on each other. In some instances this may even be true, but not usually. Most of the time the decisions made in one part of the company have repercussions for other sectors or have significant impacts on total company policy.

The problem for resolution, then, is how to maintain top-level control without stifling the initiative of talented and energetic lower managers. The answer is simple in concept but difficult in practice. To successfully resolve this problem, top management must make a concentrated effort to understand the basic dynamics of how its company functions. It must clearly define which decisions require personal top-level attention, which decisions require only general policy guidelines, and which decisions should be left to the man on the spot at each level of authority. It is well worth the time and the concentration required to insure that the company is operating with a decision-making matrix that carefully balances the need for overall management control with a need to allow lower-management-level personnel to operate with sufficient freedom to exercise their talents and their ingenuity to the maximum extent possible. And finally, notwithstanding all the above, let it be understood that in a dynamic organization there are no finite resolutions. The point is that periodic reappraisals are required to let management know how it is managing—to what extent its weaknesses and strengths are affecting the balance of power in the firm.

6

COMMUNICATIONS IN THE FIRM
Some Vital Aspects

All of us, at one time or another, experience feelings of deep frustration because of our inability to communicate a thought, an idea, or an emotion to another person or a group of people. This difficulty is pervasive. It may involve a father speaking to a son, a husband speaking to his wife, or the president of the United States speaking to the American people. Whether the method of communication is verbal, written, or graphic, the problem persists, because whatever is heard or read or seen is perceived through each individual's separate consciousness. At the same time that an individual is receiving data, his mind is already reacting to it, interpreting it, molding it—all in accordance with his own dispositions. Much of this instantaneous reaction is not even conscious. To expect people to react with total objectivity to data, particularly if the data have evocative emotional content, is to ask them, in many cases, to wipe out a lifetime of experience.

A related problem comes from the fact that in a verbal discussion that has emotional content, it is not always easy to hear the other fellow out. Even when one has the civility to let the other speaker finish his thought, it often means that the listener is simply waiting for the flow of sound to end so that an appropriate reply, which is being simultaneously formed in his mind, may be made. Hearing somebody out is not necessarily the same as listening to what is being said. If a reply is being framed in the mind of the listener while the speaker is still developing his ideas, it is likely that a true communication is not taking place. Often, after what appears to be a good meeting, when people leave satisfied with the thought that an exchange of views has taken place, the true source of satisfaction comes from the thought "I really got my idea across."

Aside from the barrier to communications that comes from the fact that any communication above the message level is likely to have emotional content and, consequently, to evoke instantaneous mental reactions, there is another significant hindrance: the appalling ambiguity of language. Even though language is the primary means of intelligent communication, it is really an inadequate tool. First, because words in themselves are charged with emotional content; second, because words are not always adequate to describe ideas precisely. Perhaps more accurately, most of us do not have the capability to combine words in such a way as to adequately describe complex ideas or situations.

One-to-one communication is difficult enough. Much more difficult is the maintenance of a constant transmission of ideas, plans, instructions, queries, answers, arguments, and resolutions in a complex business organization consisting of hundreds or thousands of individuals of different generations and diverse backgrounds. The same psychological and mechanical communications difficulties that exist between and among individuals outside an organizational environment are also found within such an environment. The same ambiguity of language that prevails in interpersonal dialogue outside the organizational framework prevails within that framework, where it is compounded manyfold by the need for second-hand and third-hand transmissions of the same information, often of a complex nature. It is probably no exaggeration to say that faulty communications cause as much damage to performance in an industrial firm as any other troublesome factor.

Communications, then, vital as they are to the life of the business organization, have certain formidable and inherent limitations. This makes it all the more important not to create or to tolerate avoidable weaknesses in communication patterns. If it is clearly recognized that even the best process of communications is intrinsically difficult, the intelligent management group will concentrate its efforts on easing the communications process within the firm to the maximum extent possible.

To accomplish this purpose, it is first of all necessary to recognize that the state of communications in the enterprise is a matter of attitude, not technique. Speaking and writing skills, after all, may be as easily used for obscuring the truth as for revealing it. This does not refute the plain fact that clear and simple language should be used in all communications, written and verbal. It is also a fact that skills and techniques of communication are sadly lacking, even among individuals with advanced levels of formal education. But to construe this as the essence of the problem of communications in business, or in any other application, for that matter, is to focus on the tip of the iceberg.

In order to probe the mass beneath the surface, this chapter will bring into focus four major factors that determine the effectiveness level of communications in the business firm. First to be considered is the pattern of informal communications between and among top-level and middle-level managers; second is the relationship between business managers at all levels and their subordinates. Finally, we will review the role of company business plans and of management information systems as vehicles for effective intracompany communications.

THE PATTERN OF INFORMAL COMMUNICATIONS

Any policy or attitude that blocks the free flow of legitimately required information is bad for a firm. Nevertheless, a general atmosphere conducive to the withholding of information can often be traced to the very top levels of the company. The interpersonal communication relationships among top-level staff and line managers can be the determining factor in setting the communication patterns of the total business. The way the key people communicate among themselves is likely to determine how their respective subordinate organizations communicate with each other. The more informal and free communications are at the top, the better will be the flow of relevant information at the succeeding lower levels of the business structure.

Ideally, management people in a business organization should make a practice of immediate verbal sharing of important and relevant information among themselves. This pattern of informal, easy communication is characteristic of many business organizations. On the other extreme, there are situations where managers hardly communicate at all and where the informal communications network operates basically by grapevine. Each of these situations reveals much about the general nature and condition of the business organization with respect to communications as well as in other areas. Consider your own organization. Do the top executives feel free to visit each other's offices for informal discussion? If a problem arises between executives or between their organizations, will the natural reaction be to meet and resolve the issues by talking them out, or will a formal memo be written, even though offices may only be separated by a few feet or a few yards? How often do top staff members communicate with each other during the course of working hours outside of staff meetings? Are there channels open for the informal exchange of ideas? At staff meetings, is there an atmosphere of tension and wariness, or are those occasions looked upon as opportunities to coordinate efforts and exchange ideas? Is it common for an executive to complain to another about a grievance against a third, or are dissatisfactions directly communicated with the object of clearing the air?

The Importance of Mutual Trust

The basic requirement for achieving a decent pattern of communications at the top levels of an organization is the existence of an atmosphere of mutual trust among the executives. An important way to establish and maintain a climate of mutual trust among managers reporting to a single chief is to resolve disagreements and problems without involving him. Certainly, an individual manager should not be placed in the position of hearing a complaint against him or his organization for the first time from his boss or at staff meetings in the presence of a larger group. This kind of surprise cannot fail to create a feeling of distrust and animosity between and among managers. The natural reaction of an executive presented with a complaint about him or his organization by his boss is to wonder why the complainer did not first come to him with the problem.

There are various patterns of behavior that may occur in relation to high-level interdepartmental problems. A given staff member, say the controller, may have had a problem within his organization that adversely affected the performance of another staff member, let us say, the vice president of manufacturing. In this situation, the controller may discuss this problem with his colleague, the vice president of manufacturing, admit to his group's responsibility for whatever damage had been caused, and indicate what he planned to do to avoid a recurrence of the problem. Or he may simply ignore the problem, hoping it will disappear or, if it doesn't, that he will be able to explain away the difficulty and somehow shift the blame from his organization.

If the controller chooses the first alternative and discusses the issue with his fellow executive, then the vice president has two basic alternatives. He can take immediate steps to minimize the damage, confident that the controller, in turn, will see to it that the initial cause of the problem is remedied. (If the damage created by the problem in the controller's office is so great that the boss has to be informed because of widespread or significant consequences, then both executives might define the problem, evaluate its consequences, and together present the issue to their superior, along with a proposed solution.) The other possibility would be for the vice president, when informed by the controller of the problem, to listen impassively, perhaps even giving the impression of being vaguely sympathetic, but at the same time limiting further communication on the issue. He might then, on a unilateral basis, carry the problem to the boss, pointing out that though the damage was to his organization, the problem originated elsewhere.

The constructive pattern of behavior, of course, is the one where both affected executives work together to resolve the issue, the one accepting responsibility and indicating his proposed "fix," the other working to minimize the damage; and, if necessary, both men taking the problem to the boss. The immature approach would be for the controller, first of all, to ignore the problem or to try to shift the blame and/or for the vice president of manufacturing to run with the story to the boss to be sure that no undeserved blame is attached to his group.

In an organization where it is normal for staff members to work out their problems among themselves, a feeling of mutual trust is bound to evolve. This in turn is the most important basis for an atmosphere of free and honest communication. On the other hand, it is obvious that where problems within an individual group are routinely passed on to high authority by leaders or members of other groups, there will be a reluctance to communicate on an honest basis. Wherever staff relationships are characterized by defensiveness and secretiveness, it is very unlikely that meaningful communications can exist.

The Impact at Lower Levels

It is highly probable that if an atmosphere of distrust prevails at the highest levels of the organization, not only will communications be stifled at that level, but the same condition will filter down to pervade lower levels of management as well. If communications are easy among the leaders of the firm, channels of communication are apt to be informal, speedy, and effective throughout the organization. As an example, if the controller communicates easily with the head of manufacturing, there is a good chance that the controller will feel free to approach directly any manager or other lower-level management person in the manufacturing area for information, rather than have to make a formal request to his peer executive and wait for the information to move down and up the organization charts and finally across at the top. To the extent that such an atmosphere of confidence prevails, cross-departmental channels of communication at all levels are likely to be free and unclogged. (For such a pattern of communications to operate successfully, it is important for the bypassed executive to receive feedback from his subordinates if the matter at hand is significant.)

The Top Manager and Communications

There are not many areas where a high-level manager can directly, on a day-to-day basis, affect the destiny of his organization. However, the one area, perhaps the most crucial, where he can exert such influence is in the realm of communications. Here he can set the pattern for good or for ill. Above all, it is finally the top manager who must set the tone for the quality and level of communications in his unit. The leader who can accept unpleasant information in a rational manner without recriminations and threats toward his subordinates is likely to become aware of significant problems as they require his attention. The boss who cannot react objectively is going to find things out late, perhaps too late to take appropriate action while a situation can still be remedied. As a result, he will probably find himself to be one of the poorest informed men in his organization. Nobody at any level enjoys the experience of being subjected to verbal abuse, and the natural tendency of most people, even the strongest of people, is to avoid or postpone such experiences until the last possible moment.

The chief executive, or any supervisor or manager, for that matter, who recognizes himself to be isolated from his subordinates might well evaluate himself from the standpoint of his reactions to the people who work for him during the course of high-pressure situations. If he reacts to unwelcome news in a threatening, irrational manner, not only will he isolate himself from his organization, but he is bound to stimulate an atmosphere of fear and unease among his closest collaborators. In such a situation, communications will be stifled or distorted. Then, once the habit of suppressing problems is developed at the higher levels of the organization, it has a tendency to spread like a contagious disease throughout the total unit.

Another habit destructive to communications is reflected in the tendency of some business leaders to communicate dissatisfaction with subordinates through the medium of uninvolved third parties. This abdication of responsibility is a result of natural reluctance to face up to the need for unpleasant personal encounters. To hear from a fellow executive of the boss's displeasure must come to the affected individual as an unsettling surprise. The first reaction might be one of disbelief. The second might well be resentment at a boss not candid enough to express his thoughts and feelings directly. Finally, and most important, the affected subordinate will probably lose confidence in the validity of any face-to-face communication with his superior. This kind of credibility gap can have only negative effects on the communications process at the higher levels of the firm.

The leader of a business unit may play a negative role in determining the tone and quality of the organization's informal communications network in still another way. Certain high-level executives seem to have the idea that a sound management technique is to play off one subordinate against the other. This may be accomplished by casually passing on derogatory remarks that one executive might have made about a peer. Or it might be done by bestowing praise on one staff member while denigrating another in the presence of either or both of them. It might be accomplished by fostering an atmosphere conducive to intrastaff intrigue.

This approach of setting staff members against each other may be rationalized by the idea that competition and rivalry bring out the best in business executives. The real motive, on the other hand, is more likely to derive from the feeling that so long as staff members can be kept fighting each other, they won't singly or collectively be working against the boss. Whatever the motivation, however, the result is contrary to the best interests of the firm. If the top men, supposedly the most valuable and creative, are expending their talents in a series of internecine battles, the potential creative thrust of the organization is being dissipated in a manner that can only be damaging to the organization. Men who look upon each other with suspicion and distrust are not likely to communicate in a meaningful way. Executives who are preoccupied with the problem of how to get a "leg up" on the next fellow are not inclined to pool their efforts for the benefit of the organization unless that benefit happens accidentally to coincide with their own narrow interests.

Keeping the Door Open

Aside from the obvious importance of establishing and maintaining open channels of communication among business managers, there is a less apparent but equally important benefit to be derived from cultivating the habit of open communications. There are few business managers who have not felt the temptation under conditions of unusual pressure to slam shut the doors of their offices and withdraw from contact with their associates.

The individual who thus isolates himself, actually or figuratively, does not see the help outside his door, but, rather, perceives a hostile and disturbing environment composed of individuals who want nothing more than to do him in. The basic problem with this kind of inward turning under pressure is that it causes a loss of perspective. The trusted fellow manager of yesterday suddenly becomes today's hostile stranger. The erstwhile loyal, capable subordinate takes on the image of a bungling idiot, indifferent to his boss's problems.

The manager who shuts off channels of communication under conditions of unusual stress or pressure loses the ability to cope with the problems that overwhelmed him in the first place. In a more rational state, the first reaction of a good manager to a heavy influx of complex or troublesome tasks is to establish priorities and delegate responsibility and work. But the manager who reacts by withdrawing closes himself off from his normal sources of assistance. For how can responsibility be delegated to "hostile outsiders"?

This kind of withdrawal represents the ultimate communications breakdown in a business environment. It is an instinctive reaction to what appears to be a threatening situation. Managers who have cultivated the habit of communicating and who routinely work hard at keeping channels open are in the best position to overcome the temptation to withdraw under conditions of pressure.

It is for this reason that the simple practice of frequent communications among business colleagues often transcends in importance even the content of such exchanges. The ability to communicate in times of individual or group stress will compensate in the long run for any time lost as a result of making time for frequent discussions, even if these discussions do no more than merely keep communication channels open.

COMMUNICATING WITH TOMORROW'S MANAGERS

Up to this point, the discussion has centered on the patterns of communication among top-level and middle-level managers. It has been pointed out that effective communications involve much more than technical language skills. The ability to communicate ideas clearly certainly eases the communication process. But equally important to the process is the communication of attitudes. When a person's attitude seems to belie his words, no matter how well spoken, it is the message conveyed by the attitude that will prevail. The manager who conveys the idea that his door is always open but shows irritation or impatience when the invitation is accepted loses credibility. The leader who indoctrinates his subordinates with the idea of organizational loyalty but foregoes loyalty for the sake of expediency nullifies his own message. Credibility is the keystone of all communications. When performance and words don't match, the effect of the words can only be counterproductive.

The establishment of a reputation for credibility is important in all interrelationships in the business unit. It is especially important in the relationship between established managers and young people who have recently entered or are about to enter the management work force. This is so because the young are drawn from colleges and universities that have been experiencing much ferment in recent years. Certainly agitation on college campuses has abated. There is now a tendency for college students to turn inward and to focus more specifically on the demands of their curriculums. This does not mean, however, that the critical attitudes toward old values and toward established authority have lost their significance. The fundamental sources of these attitudes are too deeply rooted in our recent history to disappear.

The Challenge to Authority

What are the attitudes that young people are carrying forward with them into the business world? One stands out as both a major problem and a major opportunity: a distrust of and a questioning of authority.

One of the most dramatic aspects of campus agitation during the late sixties was the ordeal of top-level college administrators, college presidents in particular. Faced with an almost unprecedented challenge to their authority by student bodies, leading college administrators failed to withstand the challenge. During the immediate post-World War II period, with the rapid growth of college and university enrollments and with the enormous physical expansion of facilities, university presidents became accustomed to the easy exercise of great authority. Their greatest challenges involved coping with growth, dealing with state legislatures (the state universities), manipulating alumni associations, raising funds, and adept handling of university politics. These were the requirements of the times, and it was the talents and skills to cope with these requirements that were cultivated by university administrators. In turn, people who possessed such talents were sought to fill these top-level positions —good administrators, master builders, capable fund raisers. In many cases, those who were chosen to head the great universities remained remote from their student bodies, isolated from them by academic administrators and faculty.

Against this background, it is not difficult to understand why many leading university presidents of the sixties were unequipped to face the challenges to their authority that came from student bodies totally dissimilar to those of the post-World War II period. The postwar students, many of them war veterans, considered the university as a place to prepare themselves for affluent, successful careers. The time spent in educational institutions was considered a transitional period. The needs of those students were in tune with the goals and capabilities of the individuals who headed the colleges and universities.

More recently a different kind of student body has emerged, a group that is characterized by critical and appraising attitudes toward authority—parental, political, educational. It is a group that questions the values of its elders and the judgment and motives of established authority. It is a generation, for instance, that even during adolescence has succeeded in breaking down codes of dress in high schools and junior high schools throughout the country.

What are the reasons for these overt challenges to adult

authority? They are intimately connected with the social tensions and pressures with which the establishment has been having such difficulty.

It is, of course, not a new thing in history for the weaknesses of established leaders and institutions to become apparent during periods of stress and change. In the past, however, these weaknesses were not so clearly spotlighted nor so easily brought into focus. The development of mass-communications media has now stripped away the protection of remoteness that public leaders have enjoyed in the past. News travels faster these days, leaving less time for officials to react to problems. Even more important, television has brought into the intimacy of the family living room the very presences of leaders forced to function under great pressure. The twitch of an eye, a slip of the tongue, a momentary loss of composure are instantly flashed to all corners of the nation. This relatively new total exposure, placed in the context of a social environment in crisis, has put public leaders very much on the defensive. The president of the United States having to think on his feet at a press conference, the head of a major corporation having to explain an embarrassing situation before a committee of Congress under the scrutiny of television cameras—these are examples of conditions that have toppled the pedestals on which public leaders formerly stood. The basic human trait of vulnerability under pressure, which was formerly hidden from the public, is now subjected to the merciless glare of an electronic eye. The result of this has been to dim the aura of authority that surrounds public leadership.

A corollary to the lessened respect for authority is the greater tendency to question judgments and decisions of the nation's decision makers. A president of the United States was humbled largely because of these new attitudes; university presidents have seen fit to resign because of their inability to cope with the challenges these attitudes represent. In effect, what has been observed is an example of the social obsolescence of powerful individuals unable to cope with the challenges of change and the need to communicate openly and directly. It is not farfetched to describe this obsolescence as also being technological in nature: for it has been the technological revolution in communications that has helped bring these leaders down.

Implications for Business Managers

What are the implications of this for the business managers of today who still plan to be exercising responsibility ten, twenty, perhaps thirty years from now?

There is very little in the background of today's managers to prepare them to cope with the work force now beginning to enter the lower levels of business management. The unquestioning acquiescence to authority that characterized the younger managers of the past is likely to be far less typical in the future. Until recently, the maverick, the questioner, has by and large been viewed as a disruptive influence. Industrial psychology tests have often served to screen him out as a danger to the stability of the business organization.

It is no doubt true that the individual incapable of accepting authority or of working with people harmoniously is a disruptive influence. However, there is no reason to believe that questioners and challengers as a group fit into this category, though certain superficial resemblances may be apparent on the surface. The chronic rejecter of authority is not interested in the rights and the wrongs of his superiors' judgments. He is essentially narrow-minded and dogmatic. The questioner, on the other hand, wants to know the whys of things. He is unwilling to give blind obedience. A whole generation of questioners is now entering the industrial management labor market. They stem from a generation that has been questioning authority probably from the time of late adolescence. Not only is it important for management to recognize this new phenomenon because it may represent a powerful trend; it is even more important because this new attitude may be one of the most constructive things that has happened to American industry in all its dynamic history.

It is suggested that the business manager who is surrounded by subordinates critical in attitude and analytical in approach has available to him a resource group of incalculable value. The business environment in which this challenging attitude is allowed to flourish is less likely to produce serious errors in judgment and thoughtless decisions. The manager faced with the challenge of intellectually alert subordinates and able to communicate with them will be forced to keep himself alert and current, thus protecting himself against early obsolescence.

Readiness to answer the question "why" when posed by a subordinate will prepare the business manager to answer this same question when posed by superiors.

The manager without the intellectual and emotional stamina to cope with questioning employees will still be able to find acquiescent, conformist, incipient yes-men to staff his subordinate positions. Such a manager, however, and his acquiescent team are likely to be losers in the tough, unpredictable years of change that will confront American industry in the future.

Notwithstanding the emergence of less docile lower management cadres, the traditional role of higher management will remain intact in the years ahead. Managers will still have to exercise authority, to make decisions, and to accept responsibility for the decisions that they make. Managers will still require the support and the loyalty of their subordinates—a challenge that leaders have had to face throughout history.

The Establishment of Credibility

The manager who wishes to win and maintain the loyalty of a newly developing management cadre needs to remember and apply a basic principle of leadership and communications —he must first gain their trust and their respect. This is an elementary idea, but it has a significant ramification: It is precisely the lack of trust and respect for authority that in great measure defines the postwar generation. How is the business manager (a bad-guy symbol to the new generation) suddenly to overcome the distrust and suspicion of which he has become a focal point? The answer is that it is easier to be distrustful and suspicious of a stereotype than of a specific human being whose humanity must be confronted daily. The young employee, warily observing his new boss, will sooner or later have to deal with the reality of the boss's personality. To the extent that this reality does not match the stereotype, the new employee will have to revise his own attitudes if *he* is not to become an obsolete figure, even in his youth.

The business leader capable of exercising elementary principles of leadership is in an excellent position to establish clear channels of communication with his younger employees. This is true because the post-Vietnam generation, by and large, has been starved for believable adult leadership models. At least in this sense the youth of today may be described as a "deprived" generation. What are the leadership characteristics required to fulfill this need in today's business environment?

- Honest, two-way, person-to-person communication
- Downward loyalty under pressure
- Readiness to respect the ideas and personality of the subordinate

Very often these basic leadership principles have been notable for their absence. This is because the pressures of operating in a business environment have made these ideas, so simple and obvious in concept, difficult to implement. It may require a major reorientation of much supervisory and management thinking to recognize their practical value. It is useful, therefore, to consider these principles in more detail.

Honest person-to-person communication
There is a belief among many business managers that it is necessary to maintain a spirit of aloofness in order to insure the respect of subordinates. This belief is based on the idea that aloofness prevents others from taking undue liberties. However, the individual who is so insecure about the core of his own personality that he must insulate himself from the humanity that surrounds him is probably not suited to function in a leadership capacity, certainly not in the decade of the seventies. The person who dehumanizes himself in this manner, who transforms his image from that of an individual to one of the stereotype, will have great difficulty in winning the loyalty or the respect of anybody, subordinates or superiors. He may protect himself from some bruising encounters; but in the process, he is also severely handicapping himself in his ability to perform as a manager.

On the other hand, the manager who is capable of and willing to communicate with his subordinates on a person-to-person basis, unafraid to demonstrate his humanity, is apt to receive a response in kind. Mutual recognition is an important step toward mutual understanding, which in turn provides a basis for mutual respect, which in turn lays the foundation for reciprocal loyalty and effective communications.

Loyalty under pressure

It is generally accepted that good business management requires that the leader offer strong support to his subordinates. The reasons for this are clear. A major portion of the manager's function is performed through the delegation of responsibility and work to his subordinates. To the extent that employees do not have the backing of their boss, their ability to function effectively is undermined, particularly when a task requires the cooperation of others. And if the job done by a subordinate is not accomplished effectively, it is ultimately his leader who fails.

In addition, and no less important, the amount of self-confidence with which a subordinate performs his function is in direct relationship to the support that he feels will be forthcoming from his boss. This is particularly true when the task at hand involves differences of opinion with others. The subordinate who lacks self-confidence is apt to exercise poor judgment in situations involving controversy. For these reasons, it is no more than simple common sense for managers to maintain as high a level of individual and organizational confidence as is possible.

In specific situations, however, these guidelines tend to become blurred. Let us assume, for instance, that within a given manager's department a serious error has been made by one or more subordinates and that this error has come to the attention of higher management. The responsible manager will probably be called upon to explain the reasons for the error made within his group. The atmosphere in his boss's office is likely to be less than pleasant, particularly if serious consequences have resulted from the mistake. The boss may even exhibit some feelings of vindictiveness. This is a scenario that every experienced manager who has ever been in trouble can easily call to mind. He may also recall the temptation to place himself outside the situation by focusing blame on the person or persons who were the direct cause of the problem.

On second thought, the real leader dismisses this temptation despite the pressure of the moment. He recognizes that placing blame on subordinates is unacceptable management behavior.

It is unacceptable primarily because regardless of who has actually made the mistake, it is the manager who is responsible for the work of his subordinates. Sooner or later, any employee with an important job to do is going to commit an error of significant consequence. People with small jobs make mistakes of little consequence; people with more responsible jobs make mistakes of greater consequence. It is not, therefore, the seriousness of a particular error that should determine the fate of a subordinate —the seriousness of an individual error can often be just a matter of bad luck. It is the employee's overall batting average that should determine his supervisor's attitude toward him.

Second, the manager faced with the temptation to extricate himself from a bad situation by transferring blame should recognize that whatever relief he gains as a result is more apparent than real. In the long run, there is no way for a chronic buck passer to escape the consequences of the actions of those who work for him. It is his job to evoke good performance. If he does not succeed in doing this, he will be judged accordingly. The real result of passing blame downward in any given situation can only be a loss of respect by superiors and subordinates alike. The manager who becomes known among his subordinates as disloyal under pressure cannot expect to maintain their loyalty in return.

The only situation in which personalizing the blame has any justification is when some unfortunate subordinate has made an error as a result of directly contravening the instructions of his boss. Even in such a case, however, the manager should consider all relevant factors, including the subordinate's basic motivations and his overall record of performance, before taking the demeaning step of transferring blame. On all counts, therefore, the habit of buck passing is bad business for the responsible manager.

Further, the manager with insight will recognize that there are some benefits to be derived even when he is called on the carpet. If he can easily accept responsibility for the performance of his organization when things have not gone well, in all probability he will be appraised as a courageous person. No matter what else happens in the situation, the impression of his attitude under pressure will be lasting.

In summary, the manager who develops the reputation for courage under pressure and for the ability to protect his people in conditions of adversity is the one most likely to receive the loyalty of his subordinates. Downward loyalty will almost inevitably result in upward loyalty. The manager who understands this two-way street and behaves accordingly has taken a long step toward asserting a position of strong leadership.

Respect for the ideas of subordinates
The ability to deal with subordinates on a person-to-person basis, to show understanding and demonstrate loyalty, forms the stepping-stones to the development of mutual respect. However, in addition to demonstrating these traits, the effective manager must be prepared to maintain an open mind in his discussions with the people who work for him. The most valuable assets that his subordinates can put at his disposal are their judgment, their experience, and their talent. For a manager to make full use of these resources, he must provide an environment for his subordinates that makes them feel intellectually at ease. The atmosphere prevailing during discussions should be such that all participants feel that their minds are in communication and that their ideas are not restricted by their positions on an organizational chart. It is through such free encounters that patterns of mutual esteem develop and foundations of mutual loyalty are strengthened.

The manager need exercise authority only when the time has come to make a decision. Once issues have been fully aired, it is unlikely that the decision he finally reaches will be resented or opposed. Most of the time (unless personal matters are at stake), it is not the decision that is resented or resisted by subordinates, but the manner in which the decision was reached and the way it was communicated.

THE COMPANY PLAN AS A COMMUNICATIONS RESOURCE

Before moving on to the vital role of management information systems as instruments of communication, one underutilized resource needs to be highlighted: the company plan. The company business plan was described earlier as a simulation of projected experience. In other words, a firm's short-range planning documents—the data that project a company's goals for a year ahead—should constitute a calendar of future events and a description of the time-phased activities that will lead to the accomplishment of these events. If the plan is realistic and sufficiently detailed, it has the potential of serving as a valuable aid to intracompany communications, provided its contents are disseminated among all operating levels of the organization. If the personnel in the firm understand the plan in total and if they know what has to happen to make the plan a reality, they will be in a much better position to understand their place in the accomplishment of the plan's objectives. They will also be in a much better position, consequently, to comprehend the instructions and communications that they will receive. A detailed understanding of the business plan among those whose job it is to convert the plan to reality can be of assistance in insuring that individual communications are not misunderstood, because these communications can then be evaluated within the context of their basic purposes. Possession of this kind of knowledge can compensate in many situations, even for incomplete or unclear instructions or communications.

Too often, the operating personnel and organizations in a company supply their respective inputs to the company plan and then hear nothing more about them. When this happens, only a small part of the potential value of the plan is realized. Although the top levels of management may have in the planning documents a valuable tool to work with when they review the total plan, the rest of the firm's personnel are often left to operate in the dark, without the understanding and the motivation that can lead to cooperative effort in the accomplishment of well-understood, mutual objectives.

The segmentation of function that is characteristic of corporate organizational structures is an inherent barrier to communication, since it tends to emphasize the bits and pieces of individual jobs and, consequently, does not provide for an understanding of the overall corporate task. But the company plan, in addition to serving as a guide for management, can do much to alleviate the problem of corporate depersonalization. It can first make clear what the business organization is trying to achieve; second, it can show how the firm intends to accomplish its objectives; and third, it can define for the individual employee his personal role in accomplishing these objectives, thus rendering him a dynamic force rather than a depersonalized cog in a machine. By understanding his role, the individual employee is better attuned to receive communications and to transmit them.

It is suggested here that personnel in the firm at all levels and in all functions—administrative, technical, salaried, hourly—should be given a clear understanding of the basic outline of the company's plan. For example, it can be as important for the hourly rated machine operator to know why the plan provides for him to increase his production from forty to forty-five pieces an hour as it is for the salesman to know why his sales quota has been increased by ten percent. If the hourly employee can see that his anticipated contribution can help his company achieve greater market penetration, he is less apt to believe he is being pushed solely for the benefit of the stockholders. He is more likely to understand that he is working to protect his own job security. The thought may also occur to him that increased labor productivity can help his union representatives bargain for a better pay and fringe package at the next scheduled negotiations with management.

The case of the hourly rated employee is an example of the relevance of planning information as a means of communication. Unfortunately, many firms have in effect given up the attempt to communicate seriously with their unionized hourly employees. This has come about because of the idea among business leaders that whereas administrative or technical or clerical or other white-collar, nonunionized personnel are loyal to their company, unionized hourly employees are loyal primarily to their unions. Frequently there is substantial basis for this idea. However, it seems clear that company loyalty and union loyalty should not be incompatible. If the hourly employee is permitted to get a clear picture of how he, through his job function, fits into the company's plans, he will be better able to visualize the synthesis between his own personal interests, the union's interests, and the interests of the firm. But this can only happen if company management has not given up by default the duty to maintain communications with its unionized hourly personnel.

The company plan, then, has a significant role to fulfill as a medium of communications between top management and all levels of personnel. It can highlight the basic interdependence among the various organizations and functions that constitute the firm, and it can give employees an insight into how their efforts are interwoven to form the fabric of a unified organization working toward common objectives.

USE AND ABUSE OF MANAGEMENT INFORMATION SYSTEMS

Management information systems (MIS) provide the channels through which information flows on a regular basis throughout the modern business corporation. They are at the heart of formal communications networks. They define company status, they measure performance, and they point out problem areas, providing the basis for corrective action. They are also often the cause of much frustration, bitterness, and distrust among the very individuals and groups they are supposed to serve. It is a common complaint that official reports emanating from management information systems are misleading; that they are difficult to understand; that they are cumbersome; and that they are inaccurate. Why do such problems persist when there is general agreement about the importance of formal reporting systems to the effective management of complex enterprises?

The crux of the issue is a widespread failure to perceive that management information systems are essentially instruments of communication, subject to all the "human" problems and complexities that characterize other forms of communication. In general, communications problems are usually perceived as "human," to be dealt with by communications experts, psychologists, industrial relations personnel, and similar highly verbal types. Difficulties emanating from formal reporting systems are thought of as technical, or "nonhuman," to be handled by systems analysts, controller personnel, and computer experts trained to deal with such subject matter as data collection, systems logic, and the like.

Many aspects of formal reporting are indeed technical in nature. However, these aspects are secondary and are becoming increasingly routine. They are essentially related to the input of information to the system: its internal logic, the accuracy and flow of the raw data, the compatibility of hardware and software, the appropriate choice of computer configuration.

The communications aspect of reporting systems is related to systems output: the information generated by the system, and the part of the system with which the user comes into contact. It is in this regard that management information systems experience their notable failures. The main cause of these failures is that systems analysts, controller personnel, and computer technicians are concerned primarily with systemization, not with communication. What is important to them is not the ends of the system but the system itself. It is not really surprising, therefore, that the basic function of MIS as a communications tool is only incidentally addressed.

The Development of MIS: Confusion of Means and Ends

Why does this confusion of means and ends still prevail in complex and sophisticated business organizations despite the widespread dissatisfaction with information systems? To understand why this situation exists, it is worth a brief review of the origin of reporting systems in the modern business firm.

Long before the development of extensive business information systems and the computer as aids to business management, two basic reports constituted the core of business reporting: the balance sheet and the profit and loss statement. Today these two documents still present the ultimate summary picture of company condition and performance. Notwithstanding the many pages of other financial data presented in the annual reports of public companies, these financial statements are still at the heart of even the most elaborate multicolored, many-pictured annual report. The balance sheet informs the stockholder of the point-in-time condition of his company: its net worth, its relative liquidity, its long-term debt, its ownership structure (what the company owns and what it owes). The profit and loss statement tells how the company performed during the previous fiscal period: the charges that it incurred; the revenue that it received; and the profits or losses that resulted. The chief communicators of company condition and performance, through preparation of the basic business reports, were, and to a major extent still are, the company accountants. (The only operational business reports that are generally recognized as instruments of communication, that is, where the sensibilities and reactions of report receivers need to be reckoned with, are the balance sheet and profit and loss statement as they appear in annual reports for the benefit of stockholders. It is interesting that media experts are used extensively in the preparation of corporate annual reports.)

The second development of modern reporting systems is also a contribution of the accounting profession. The increasing complexity and diversity of companies and their products established the need to know, not only total costs and total revenues of a firm, but the costs of individual products and services, and even of components and increments of products and services. This led to the development of cost accounting that identified costs to their detailed points of origin. In parallel there developed a new class of professionals, the efficiency experts, who wanted not only to identify costs but to find ways to reduce them by improving work methods. Whole families of performance reports developed from this new requirement. Finally came the systems analysts and the computer with its technicians to rationalize and speed the process of data collection and data reporting. Undoubtedly, the first problems associated with these advances in the state of the art of business information were technical in nature. The advances were made by technicians, and the associated problems had to be solved by them. The focus naturally had to be on the systems, but with the resultant neglect of the system users.

It was this concentration on improving the technical state of the art that led to the confusion of means and ends in the development of management information systems. It is because of this confusion that so much controversy still surrounds the issue of formal reporting in the business firm. It is not unusual to find still in use, alongside elaborate computer-based reports, unofficial reporting systems that use the electronically processed reports only as source data for the preparation of hand reports.

When this condition prevails, it is a clear symptom that the official reporting network, or specific segments of it, has failed as a communications medium. The degree of failure of any formal reporting system is in direct proportion to the number of supplementary or substitute reports that are generated throughout an organization. For example, when a high-level manager spends a large proportion of his time plotting graphs from data he received in formal reports, or when a shop foreman sits at his desk working on his own private tote sheets when he should be out on the floor supervising his employees, indications are that the formal information system is failing to perform its function. When management or supervisory personnel are periodically surprised by adverse developments, despite the fact that such developments have been signalled by the information system, the implication is that though the pertinent data were available, they were not effectively communicated.

Once it is recognized that the lack of effectiveness of formal reporting systems is essentially a failure in communications, it becomes possible to identify the real problems and to look for solutions by refocusing on the essentials of good communication.

Communicating Through MIS: Basic Factors

What are the essentials of good communication and how do they apply to formal business reporting? They are credibility (trust), timeliness, clarity (comprehensibility), and relevance. These are the characteristics that identify *any* healthy communication relationship. How are these characteristics to be woven into the fabric of management reporting systems? In order to define a frame of reference that will aid in answering this question, a few basic understandings must be established: What are the objectives of a management reporting system? Who are its logical users? How should report formats be determined? How should the question of report timeliness vis-à-vis frequency be addressed?

Let us consider, in turn, each of these factors.

What are the objectives of a management reporting system?
The purposes of a management reporting system are to pro-

vide pertinent information concerning the condition of the operation, to measure the performance of individuals and groups,
and to point out present and potential problem areas for timely
corrective action. It is the eyes and the ears of an organization
too big or too complex to comprehend on the basis of direct
observation. It is the medium through which the various segments of the organization tell each other what is happening in
the day-to-day life of the firm. It ties together, in a series of
communications networks, the total organizational pyramid and
its subpyramids from apex to base, vertically and laterally and
in all other meaningful directions.

Who requires access to management reports?
Any individual in the firm whose understanding of his work
environment can be deepened and broadened by access to
organized data relating to his work activity should have access
to such data. Management and supervisory personnel who cannot gain a total understanding of their areas of responsibility by
direct observation require the aid of organized report data. It
is also true that in some situations the individual worker or work
group, operating in a highly restricted environment, may also
benefit from management reports. For instance, in plants where
the performance of machine operators or assembly workers is
measured against efficiency standards, a posted daily or weekly
efficiency report might be a useful communications tool to let
the individual worker or work group evaluate its own performance. (Such a report, of course, would have to be used with discretion, depending upon the relationship between management
and labor.)

Who should determine report formats?
It is clear that different management levels and diverse
functions within the corporate organization require different
kinds of information from the company reporting system. The
common aspects in the multiplicity of diverse requirements
relate to the four basic factors in effective communications:
credibility, timeliness, clarity, relevance. However, once these
common aspects are agreed upon, a major question still remains:

Who should determine report formats? The systems analyst? The controller? Top management? The report user?

Ideally, each report user should determine the format of reports produced for his benefit. After all, different individuals have different ways of perceiving reality. It is rarely feasible, however, to tailor reports to suit each individual's preferences. But before we regretfully discard the idea, it is worth observing that if individually tailored reports were possible, three of the four criteria for good communications would be immediately achievable: credibility, clarity, and relevance. If a user were able to participate in the design of his own report, if he understood how the data were gathered, if he could choose what went into it—he would surely find such a report credible, clear, and relevant.

Well, is it, after all, totally impossible for report users to participate in the design of their own reports? That depends on the number of users. At the apex of each organizational pyramid there is usually a single individual. Surely, he should have the privilege of having access to data in the form that he wants them. Some top managers gain most from summarized data. Others prefer extensive detail. Why not recognize that report preferences are largely a matter of taste, like clothes, food, and haircuts?

As we move progressively down the management pyramid, the issue of report format preference becomes more complex. The more personnel to be found at a given reporting level in the same general function, the more likely the diversity of taste. And the more unfeasible it becomes to give each responsible leader a report tailored to his own preferences. For instance, in an organization with twenty foremen at a given level of supervision, whose information needs are approximately the same, it is not feasible to provide each one of them with data in his preferred format.

In view of this practical limitation, what can be done to satisfy the total user group of the credibility, clarity, and relevance of the data that they receive from the management information system? A workable, if not perfect, solution is to have the total user group or a committee of the group (depending on the number of users) participate with the systems analyst in the design of reports prepared for their mutual use. Such a procedure will require compromise and accommodation among the users. But it has the major advantages of pooling operating knowledge, providing a report that has user-group approval (though not ideal for each individual), and developing lines of communication between staff and line personnel.

This last benefit should not be minimized. By acting as a technical consultant for a committee of operating people, the staff man—systems analyst, procedures specialist, controller representative—has an opportunity to demonstrate his own usefulness and credibility as a corporate contributor.

There is another approach to the development of reporting systems. This is based on the idea that experienced systems analysts are most capable of designing report systems and should be given total responsibility for producing the end product. Then, it is maintained, if the resultant system or report has the full support of top management, the users can be indoctrinated in its use.

There are serious deficiencies in this approach. First of all, it is fallacious to assume that a relative outsider is more capable of determining the report needs of operating personnel than are the personnel themselves. The practical experience of potential users, their "feel" for what they need to help them manage, is bound to be more realistic than the views of a systems analyst (inside staff man or outside consultant) notwithstanding his greater theoretical knowledge of reporting systems. Second, if the potential system users participate in its design, they are much more likely to cooperate in its implementation and to be tolerant of any bugs that appear in the early testing phases. Management information systems are most vulnerable during their early trial period, and it is then that the cooperation of potential users is most needed. A hostile user group, suspicious of the innovation that is being crammed down its throat, can seriously impede the implementation of the system or destroy it completely during its early, vulnerable stages. Third, and most important, the management information system and the reports that emanate from it are primarily communications instruments and as such must be believed, understood, and valued by the user groups. The best way to accomplish this is to make the user groups feel that the system is essentially their creation.

What, then, should the role of the systems analysts or other designated staff technicians be in the design of management information (communication) systems? They should first of all be resource people. They should make clear what is and what is not achievable in the way of a report or a reporting system. In working with user personnel, they should serve as mediators, helping the various user groups or user-group committees to work out a consensus satisfactory to the user community. Then, once format and content are resolved, the next step for the staff experts is to develop the technical aspects of the system and to stay with it until the bugs are worked out.

By engaging the interest and participation of user groups, then, it becomes possible to insure that three of the basic communications requirements mentioned earlier are woven into the fabric of the formal communications system: credibility, because the users will understand the derivation and evolution of report data; clarity, because the users will participate in developing the report formats; and relevance, because the users will build into the system data which are comprehensive and meaningful to them.

The "timeliness" syndrome

Let us now turn to the fourth criterion of effective communications as applicable to a business reporting system. On the surface, the question of "timely" reporting would appear to be beyond controversy. Who, after all, can take issue with the need for timely reporting when clear visibility is so basic a need for the efficient management of business enterprises? Unfortunately, the issue is not so easily disposed of. The concept of "timeliness" has been the source of much misdirected effort and unnecessary cost in the preparation of management reports in this computer age, when data can be prepared and disseminated with fantastic speed.

The misdirection and waste arise from a misconception concerning the meaning of the word *timeliness* in its application to business reporting. The *World Book Dictionary* offers a clue to the source of the problem. The dictionary defines *timely* as "at the right time," "opportunely," "seasonably." It also offers what it describes as archaic definitions: "early," "soon."

If it were generally recognized by management personnel, systems analysts, and computer salesmen that timely reports are those that arrive at the right time and not necessarily those that appear quickly or frequently, much of the confusion and waste caused by the demand for timely reporting would gradually fade away. As it is, there is a prevailing tendency to equate timeliness with speed and frequency. It is quite natural for computer salesmen to fall prey to and propagate this misconception. The great asset of their wonderful machines is speed—speed in calculating and speed in printing.

However, the problem with this idea, as it affects business managements, is that it often causes them to invest in computer equipment beyond their needs and to create stacks and stacks of reports that cannot and need not be assimilated as fast as they are produced. In addition, reports produced with unnecessary frequency become counterproductive. Their value becomes debased because users begin to find them burdensome and guilt producing owing to the difficulty of keeping up with them. Finally, reports that appear too frequently have the effect of blurring perspectives, because constant bombardment by data makes it difficult to sort out meanings.

Does all this mean that "real time" reports or daily reports may be categorically classified as wasteful or counterproductive? No. Not if the "real time," hourly, daily, or weekly report is opportune.

How, then, can we tell when a reporting system is turning out reports on a timely, or opportune, basis as opposed to merely quickly or frequently? Once these differences are recognized, general criteria for timeliness may be established. As an aid to approaching such criteria, let us again set out the major purposes of business information systems:

- To inform management of the current status and the overall performance level of the operation.
- To measure the performance of individuals and groups.
- To highlight present and potential problem areas so that corrective action may be taken.

With these purposes in perspective, we may review the major considerations that should be used to determine the frequency and speed of information reporting.

Time sensitivity. The reporting system first calls to the attention of management a continuing series of activities, events, and conditions that characterize the life of the organization. Some of these activities, events, and conditions are subject to rapid change, others to more gradual change. In other words, different business phenomena have different degrees of time sensitivity.

The existence of differing time sensitivities suggests one criterion of timeliness. If notable change in a particular activity, event, or condition takes place on an hourly basis, for instance, ideally "real time" reporting should be used to communicate what is happening.

Reasonable reaction time. Business managers have many things to do besides read reports and react to them. They must deal with previously identified problems, establish new directions, take care of their correspondence, attend meetings, give and receive instructions, and so on. Every business leader in an active organization has a backlog of significant things to accomplish. Therefore, before deciding that a particular work-related phenomenon should be formally reported on a daily basis, even if the phenomenon is extremely time-sensitive, the manager must first decide whether he can or should react to a change in the particular situation as soon as he becomes aware of it. Perhaps the matter could or should wait for resolution because of other priorities; or because solutions are not instantly available; or because subordinate levels, in any case, should have a first crack at the problem. No individual can judge better than the responsible official how crucial time is with respect to the receipt of certain kinds of information. However, it is worth pointing out that because a particular condition is time-sensitive, subject to quick and volatile change, it does not automatically mean that such change is so drastic in impact as to require immediate attention.

The manager who tends to demand reports on a quick and frequent basis, if he is willing to appraise himself realistically, may find that he is not really using his report data as efficiently as he originally had intended. He may find himself sweeping today's reports from his desk into the wastepaper basket to make way for tomorrow's updated versions because of the pressure of other work. When this happens, it is time to reexamine his notion of time sensitivity. Perhaps less frequent report data would serve as well or better if the lesser frequency helped separate the forest from the trees.

Importance of perspective. These considerations bring into focus a third factor in establishing a standard for timeliness with respect to management reports: perspective. As a generalization, it is true that the higher a manager is in the organizational structure, the less quickly he can react to problems called to his attention. Why? Because the problems brought to the attention of a higher-level manager are of a more fundamental nature than those dealt with by his subordinates. Otherwise they would be handled at lower levels and not come to his attention in the form of action items. When the higher manager does hear of a problem outside normal channels, before he gets involved with it he must determine whether it is a passing phenomenon, something that his subordinates will take care of. Managers who do not understand this are likely to overreact by second-guessing their subordinates on relatively minor issues. What is conveyed as friendly advice from above may easily be thought of by subordinates as harassment.

A hypothetical example may present this issue with greater clarity.

Let us say that a works manager is in charge of a factory with multiple manufacturing departments. It is the habit of this manager to receive each morning departmental efficiency reports covering the previous day's activity. It is also his practice, when a particular department shows up on a given report with less than anticipated performance for the previous day, to telephone the responsible supervisor to find out what went wrong.

The department's direct supervisor receives the same daily report, which describes the efficiency of each operator and summarizes total department efficiency. It is his job to deal with the matter of operator performance on a regular basis. When he has a problem, he knows it is his responsibility to see it through. He also knows that he will receive a telephone call from upstairs as soon as the problem shows up in the reports.

What is the feeling of the supervisor likely to be? If he is competent, aware of his responsibility and accustomed to coping with the problems of operator performance, he may resent having to divert his attention from the job in order to fill his boss in. Second, he is likely to resent being put on the defensive and kept off balance over what he considers to be a passing issue, particularly when he has a problem to concentrate on and work out. He won't really want to be thinking about his boss at all; he'll want to be working on the problem.

The boss, proud of his detailed knowledge, feels that he is keeping his subordinates on their toes. His subordinates, on the other hand, feel that they are being diverted from doing their jobs by harassment from above and that there is a lack of confidence in their ability to solve their problems.

Actually, the boss may feel no such lack of confidence. His pattern of daily follow-up, as he sees it, is simply a way of staying on top of *his* job.

In this situation, daily attention to efficiency reports at the works-manager level is clearly counterproductive—that is, unless he is reacting to a chronically bad situation and really needs to exert daily pressure on his subordinates. Under normal operating circumstances, however, a summarized weekly report for the review of the works manager would be more timely, though less frequent than a daily report covering the previous day's activity. Also, from the vantage point of a week's activity reviewed against the trend of previous weeks, the works manager could develop better perspective concerning the performance of his operating departments. The foreman confronted with questions about a negative trend is far less likely to consider himself harassed than when he is questioned about a single subnormal day. By being left undisturbed in the short run, he has the time and the frame of mind to work his way out of his problems. If poor performance persists, then, indeed, the problem becomes one for his boss.

The particular issue of timely reporting hypothesized here represents a double problem in communication. First, the daily contact with the boss by means of the performance report is representative of poor communication because the data produced are neither timely nor relevant. Second, the high-level overreaction encouraged by the too-frequent reporting is conducive to misunderstandings and tensions on the part of subordinates, who are kept off balance as a result.

It is not intended in this discussion to suggest that detail-oriented executives change their approach and become what they might consider "broad brush" managers. The issue in point is not the level of detail in management reports, which, as indicated earlier, is a matter of taste and management philosophy. Rather, it is the question of the report's timeliness as it influences communications for good or for bad. It is suggested here that the frequency of detailed review may often be decreased to the overall benefit of a business unit. What benefit? The top leaders would have more time to spend on issues of more long-range significance. Subordinate managers would feel more confident, less pressure-ridden in their jobs; they would be able to exercise better judgment in the absence of harassment from above.

If there is a single generalization to be made about the timeliness of reports emanating from a management information system, it is that the lower the management level to be served, the more frequent and detailed the reports should be. Lower-level managers, because their areas of responsibility are more limited and their problems less fundamental, can and should react quickly to problems and dislocations; and the reporting system should be geared to helping obtain such quick reactions. Correspondingly, the higher the level of responsibility, the less time-sensitive the problems, notwithstanding their greater magnitude and impact.

Are there exceptions to these generalizations about report timeliness? Certainly. What are they? That is for each management group to determine in its process of self-appraisal. Here are a few questions that the individual manager might ask himself to help him come to grips with the issue of report timeliness:

1. How much time can I effectively devote to analyzing reports?
2. How meaningful are the report data I receive that describe activities, events, and conditions over small increments of time?

3. Will any real damage be done if I miss this report for a day or a week or a month?

4. Am I infringing on the responsibilities and subverting the initiative of my subordinates by becoming overinvolved in their normal problems? If so, should I really be monitoring their activities on as frequent a basis as I have been?

7

THE PSYCHIC ENERGY LEVEL
An Index of Company Vitality

The ability of a company to set objectives, the way the company communicates, and the methods it uses to implement decisions are all basic to the success of the operation. Taken together, they constitute to a considerable extent the intellectual and administrative machinery of the firm.

These capabilities are in a sense analogous to a complex set of capital equipment at rest. The equipment may be new and well designed, or it may be old and obsolete. But regardless of condition, if it is not being driven by a suitable energy source at the appropriate energy level, it has no productive value. This is also true of the firm's intangible capital equipment—its intellectual and administrative framework. The best conceived business approaches and policies and procedures can be effective only in proportion to the collective driving force, the "psychic energy" level, of the individuals who are conducting the business of the firm. No matter how sound the company's plans, how well established its patterns of communication, how clear-cut its decision-making and decision-implementation apparatus, without a high level of psychic energy the company lacks the core ingredients for success and long-term viability. It is a matter of importance, therefore, to focus attention on this aspect of life in the firm.

DEFINING THE PSYCHIC ENERGY LEVEL

It would be a great convenience if there were available a set of gauges or instruments to evaluate the collective psychic energy of the company in terms of discrete measurements—as physicians, for instance, measure the vital signs of their patients. Unfortunately, this is not the case. It is possible, however, to define the criteria that indicate the firm's energy level and to evaluate the performance of the firm with respect to these criteria. In this chapter we shall first discuss the qualitative aspects of these criteria. We shall then propose specific quantitative indices that may be used to measure, at least in gross terms, levels of company vitality.

The general characteristics that determine the firm's vitality level are the current collective state of the art within the company, its drive to innovate (its creativity), and the power and efficiency of its follow-up practices.

For the purpose of this discussion, these characteristics are described as follows:

1. *State of the art.* The level of technical and management knowledge that the company has available to apply to its affairs, as compared with the level of knowledge throughout the industry or industries in which the company operates. Current state of the art is a result largely of the innovative drive of previous periods in company history.

2. *The drive to innovate.* The energy with which improvements in the state of the art are presently being pursued and the intensiveness of the search for new and better ways to accomplish the objectives of the firm.

3. *Power and efficiency of follow-up practices.* The relative diligence with which projects are carried through; the concentration applied to problem resolutions; the relative ability to channel new ideas into the system for appraisal and action (the relative ability to minimize the dissipation or evaporation of new

ideas derived from any source); the responsiveness of management to new proposals in terms of reaction time.

QUALITATIVE INDICES OF COMPANY VITALITY

How can the individual business unit be evaluated in terms of these characteristics or criteria? Put in the form of questions, here are some basic indices that may be used to establish the vitality level at which the firm functions.

- How powerful is the drive within the organization to lower the cost of products or services marketed by the organization?
- What has been the recent record in improving or updating products or services?
- How much product or service diversification has taken place as an outgrowth of in-house capabilities?
- What has been the company's recent record of market penetration?
- What is the firm's personnel profile and how is it changing?

These basic questions are sufficient to provide the introspective management group with a basis for evaluating the vitality, or psychic energy level, of the firm or its subunits. Let us consider each of these questions in turn.

The Drive to Lower Cost

Greater productivity, greater unit output per unit of input, is a basic objective of manufacturing and service industries. Despite this commonly held objective, there is a significant amount of variation in relative productivity within industries serving the same markets. The position of individual companies making the same or similar products or services is largely determined by the relative cost structure of those companies. This is especially true in industries that are price-competitive. However, it is also true of business organizations that compete primarily on other bases, such as product identification (cosmetics companies) or service (banks). The greater the spread between cost and revenue, the more resources there are for reinvestment or income distribution to stockholders.

Variations in productivity do not come about as a result of happenstance. They are directly related to the level of talent, ingenuity, and drive that is applied to the problem of reducing cost. There are only a few ways to reduce cost without lessening the quality (utility to end users) of products and services. The most basic of these are: reducing the amount of labor required to produce and distribute the product or service; and reducing the cost of material, by changing the material content of the product and/or buying materials and supplies at cheaper prices.

Reducing the amount of labor

The most direct way to reduce the cost of labor is to *minimize labor inefficiencies*, especially those associated with slow or careless work. The measurement of direct labor performance in the manufacture of tangible products has reached a relatively advanced state. The evolution of cost accounting, the development of time study methods, and other work breakdown techniques have made possible the comparison of actual labor costs with achievable targeted costs.

The measurement of "indirect labor" costs in factories and in service organizations is less advanced. Possibly because of the nature of administrative and clerical work, it will never be feasible to measure these activities with the degree of accuracy possible for "product-producing" labor. However, significant progress has been made in developing work-measurement approaches for indirect labor. There are consulting firms that devote substantial effort to these techniques.

A major test of company vitality is the level of effort expended and the results achieved in implementing techniques to measure employee performance. Does the cost system collect data in such a way as to make possible the measurement of performance? Are there realistic standards that actual performance can be compared with? Above all, if the answer to these questions is affirmative, is there a strong follow-through impetus in management to correct problems of labor inefficiency, or have standards of performance been allowed to erode for lack of such impetus? (Excuses are readily available to explain decline in productivity: changes in labor force quality; union problems; lack of employee loyalty.)

If performance has been allowed to deteriorate, if reasonable improvements have not been achieved, or if the business unit does not even have data to let it know the status of its labor performance, then in this area, certainly, the psychic energy level of the unit must be rated as poor in terms of state-of-the-art innovative thrust and follow-through habits.

A second and more dramatic way of reducing labor costs is to *reduce the inherent labor content* of individual products or services and of the overall business organization. Revised manufacturing processes and the substitution of equipment for personnel are the means to accomplish this purpose in manufacturing firms.

In service and administrative organizations, this objective is izing certain clerical tasks formerly performed by clerks or rela- accomplished by streamlining the flow of paperwork, computer- tively low-level administrative personnel, eliminating redundant functions, and using modern office services techniques. Banks, insurance companies, hospitals, and other service industries, as well as the administrative and clerical sections of manufacturing companies, have been active in the search for improved methods of both using personnel more efficiently and applying computer and business-machine technology.

The approach to making better use of the company work force as a means of reducing cost is essentially the same for manufacturing and service industries: to streamline the flow of work or to substitute equipment for human drudgework. In a factory such equipment might be automated assembly machinery. In a service environment it might be computers and business machines.

Whose job is it to accomplish these economies? In factories, the manufacturing or industrial engineers. In administrative and service organizations, the systems experts or office service professionals. In addition, however, the innovative business organization does not neglect to make use of the resourcefulness and experience of the general work force in coming up with cost saving ideas through the medium of formal cost-reduction plans and employee suggestion programs.

Here again, the introspective organization can test its vitality by analyzing its performance in accomplishing cost savings. How proficient are its industrial engineers, systems analysts, office service experts? Are they familiar with the current state of the art of their disciplines? What has the actual cost-reduction record been? Are formal employee suggestion programs in effect? And an important corollary—if such programs are in effect, how active is the response to them? The level of activity of a suggestion program offers an excellent indication of the extent to which non-management personnel are willing to bring an innovative spirit to their work. In addition, response to employee suggestion programs is a good barometer of the efforts made by management to stimulate innovative ideas.

Alert and creative industrial engineering groups will continually find ways to reduce labor content in their organizations. They will know the newest techniques of their profession. They will learn not only from their own experience but from equipment manufacturers, professional associations, seminars, courses, professional journals. The absence of a consistent cost-reduction program in the factory or office constitutes a negative reflection on the business unit's psychic energy level.

Reducing the cost of material

The costs of materials and components make up a significant portion of total manufacturing cost. For organizations that specialize in assembly operations and do little or no heavy manufacturing or fabrication, the cost of "buy parts" is usually the major element of total manufacturing cost.

The cost of material and components for a given product can be reduced in two ways without reducing product quality (assuming a minimum of operational waste in the form of scrap and offal). One way is to substitute less expensive but equally serviceable material for more expensive material and to eliminate nonrequired components or parts that do not affect the basic utility of the product. The other way is to use aggressive shopping methods in the purchase of required material (or operating and administrative supplies).

Material substitution. The techniques of "value engineering" (cost reduction through design change) are increasingly in use in dynamic and progressive companies. These techniques consist of organized, consistent analysis of product designs with the aim of reducing product cost without affecting product quality. Changes in materials and elimination of redundant components have had dramatic impacts in reducing both labor and material costs in military products as a result of the major emphasis placed by the U.S. Department of Defense on value engineering.

The management of manufacturing enterprises should ascertain how much effort is devoted by their industrial engineers, designers, metallurgists, and purchasing agents to finding alternate materials for or eliminating unnecessary materials and components in the products produced by the firm. How much management effort is being expended to encourage value engineering in the organization? A major criterion of the technical state of the art and of the innovative thrust within a company is the extent of and persistence with which such activities (by any name) are conducted.

Although value engineering is a concept that applied originally to manufacturing organizations, it also applies to service organizations in a somewhat modified form. Hospitals, for instance, have instituted significant cost reductions through the use of alternate materials and supplies.

Alternate sources for materials and supplies. Despite their importance, purchasing departments are often taken for granted. In fact, the operation of purchasing departments should be scrutinized with great care. Buying is a special skill with its own state of the art. Just as is true of other business functions, the level of competence, the spirit of innovation, and the ability to follow through of purchasing departments vary substantially from company to company.

In reviewing the performance of purchasing organizations, it is important to recognize that there is an understandable temptation among purchasing agents to develop and cultivate reliable groups of vendors and then to adhere closely to the use of those vendors. Vendor reliability is often construed as the supplying of material of consistent quality on time for an agreed-upon price and the provision of emergency assistance on a timely basis. When purchasing agents assemble a group of vendors who comply with these requirements, the life of the purchasing agent becomes much simpler—but at a price. The price is that this approach to purchasing may erode the market position of the firm.

The dynamic purchasing organization will assume that purchasing agents for competing companies, rather than relying on a well-established group of vendors, will be out beating the bushes in search of new vendors who will sell at lower prices. The challenge is to protect delivery and quality while at the same time seeking out price advantage by encouraging a competitive spirit among vendors.

The basic attitudes are well worth analyzing. Is there an inclination in the purchasing department to take the safe way, to develop a group of vendors and then stick with them because of their reliability? Or are the purchasing people indoctrinated with the idea of developing new sources, with the result that the proven vendors are not allowed to become complacent toward a guaranteed customer who need not be given maximum price consideration? The purchasing organization that does not seek out new sources for parts, material, and supplies on a consistent basis may be quietly and undramatically eroding the competitive position of its company. Lack of innovation and enterprise in its dealings with the vendors will give it a rating of "low" on the psychic energy level scale.

The Product Improvement Record

A product is improved when its useful life is increased or its performance enhanced. Product improvement may serve to ward off product obsolescence, it may add a competitive advantage to a product, or it may form the basis for an added market by making a somewhat better quality product available to a more affluent group of purchasers. Because the product improvement record of a company is an important gauge of its dynamism, the introspective management will therefore want to ask these questions: Should there be a group within the company with the specific function of finding ways to improve products? If there is such a group, what has its track record been? Is the total organization imbued with the idea of product improvement? If the answer is yes, ideas to improve products as well as reduce costs should emanate from all sources, not only from those with the specific responsibility to accomplish these ends.

Product Diversification

Among creative individuals one idea leads to another. In the creative business enterprise, one product should yield not only product improvements but also ideas for diversification of product or service lines. From what sources might such ideas come? From almost any activity or functional group in the firm. Product diversification could be an outgrowth of existing products. In a manufacturing firm, new ideas could develop as a result of more extensive use of the firm's basic manufacturing capability. Metal, for instance, can be bent, twisted, molded, pounded, or cut into innumerable shapes, each with different end uses.

There are also other opportunities for product diversification. Many complementary products share the same kind of marketing outlets in a very natural way, even though the products themselves may be totally dissimilar. For example, companies that manufacture lawn mowers find it practical to market garden products, such as seeds and fertilizer. Is this a feasible approach for your manufacturing or service company—that is, to search for natural marketing connections among complementary products or services? If so, has your organization been sufficiently innovative to take advantage of such connections?

The Market Penetration Record

A company's salesmen are its link to the outside world. No matter how efficient, innovative, and aggressive the rest of the company may be, ultimately the salesmen must sell the product. The rest of the company creates inventory, but the marketing department must convert the inventory to sales. In the fields of market planning, sales promotion, and direct sales effort, there is as much potential variation in creativity and drive as in any other aspect of the business. The complacent salesman, the unimaginative sales promotion staff, the short-sighted market planner—any of these can contribute significantly to the gradual decay of an otherwise healthy company. In each of these areas of marketing, the energy level requires total management attention. Fortunately, their related activities can often be directly measured in terms of results; market performance is subject to tangible measurement. This is true both in absolute terms (total sales volume) and in relative terms (share of the market), and it is important for a company to pay close attention to both aspects. Decreases in market share, notwithstanding increases in total sales, may be symptomatic of a gradually eroding position.

It also behooves management to evaluate the sales-promotion attitudes of its company as compared with those of competitors. Which is considered to be the innovator in this activity —your company or your closest competitor?

Aside from its job of bringing in business, the modern marketing department recognizes that it has a function as an intelligence-gathering group to bring into the company a constant stream of information about customer wants and needs as well as new ideas that are being introduced into the market by competitors. The company salesmen, because of their exposure to the environment of customers and competitors, should be a valuable source of information necessary to keep the firm current and responsive to the needs of rapidly changing marketplaces. If this is characteristic of your marketing organization, then it is probably functioning well in all its other aspects. However, if your marketing department presents an image of order takers and customer-relations men content to please their existing customers and to wait, pad in hand, for repeat orders, then, obviously, a serious problem exists in this area of activity.

Although the marketing department is at the opposite end of the product cycle from the purchasing department, there are striking similarities in the patterns of strength and weakness in both groups. An uninspired, complacent salesman can function happily within a reliable circle of good customers. A similarly disposed purchasing agent can function happily within a circle of acceptable, reliable suppliers. In both areas, serious long-term erosive effects can take place as a result of such passive attitudes. On the other hand, a constant search for new customers by the salesman and the continued development of new vendor sources by the purchasing agent can contribute in the one case to broader sales penetration and in the other to better prices for materials, components, supplies, and subcontract items. Like the salesman, the purchasing agent should also be a valuable source of intelligence for the company. His association with vendors should bring in information about competitors' attitudes and activities, as well as ideas for new and complementary products.

The Changing Personnel Profile

The intensity of cost reduction efforts, the product improvement thrust, achievements in product diversification, market penetration trends—these are specific indicators of company vitality levels. A more general indicator of company vitality is the company personnel profile: the basic character of the business unit's personnel complement. Analysis of changes in the basic makeup of and the evolving attitudes among the work force can provide valuable insights concerning future trends in company vitality levels. There are, of course, many characteristics that define the nature of a work force. Here we are concerned only with those that shed light on likely future levels of the state of the art: innovative energy and follow-through practices, the basic factors that determine company vitality.

The elements that we shall place in focus are personnel turnover rates, changes in composite age levels through time, and company and employee attitudes toward general, technical, and professional continuing education and training. The directions in which each of these elements are trending are significant with respect to the total work force. They are especially significant as they affect middle management cadres, however, because the vitality level of this group is a big influence on the condition of the organization at lower levels.

High rates of personnel turnover are always a source of concern among business organizations that make products or provide services based on high degrees of professional, administrative, technical, and manual skills. Under such conditions, high personnel turnover constitutes a serious resource drain, and the alert management group will pay close attention to trends as well as current rates. An unsatisfactory turnover rate should be the occasion for a careful review of company personnel policies and practices. Effective personnel departments consider it a major responsibility to prevent the erosion of capability among the company work force. (The performance of a personnel department in this regard offers significant indications about *its* vitality level.)

Generally speaking, the dangers associated with high personnel turnover are well recognized. More subtle, however, are the implications of a personnel complement that remains relatively stable through time. It would seem reasonable to conclude that if an unstable work force characterized by high turnover rates is undesirable, then a stable work force characterized by low turnover rates is desirable. The fact is, however, that this proposition is not necessarily, certainly not automatically, valid.

There is no question that a stable, loyal work force has the potential of being a powerful asset. However, work-force stability may also in its own way be erosive to the health and vitality of a business firm. This is true because even the most stable of work forces is a changing work force. As people grow older and mature, they tend to experience changes in outlook, intellectual flexibility, stamina, and initiative. This is a particularly significant factor among middle management supervisory and technical personnel who remain in place over long periods of time because their paths to further advancement may be blocked by their own limitations or by the reality of a narrowing management pyramid at higher organizational levels. It should be recognized in organizations that pride themselves on work-force stability that such stability carries with it the possibility for stagnation, because the stable work force is also an aging work force. This presents the kind of situation where success (maintenance of a stable, loyal personnel complement) may contain the seeds of future failure (stagnation, complacency, loss of initiative).

The question then becomes, how is this potential contradiction to be resolved? On the one hand, valued and loyal employees are encouraged to remain with their firms. Pension plans, salary structures, and working conditions are designed in such a way as to accomplish this end. On the other hand, an aging and maturing force is a natural consequence of a successful employee relations policy. And a frequent corollary to aging is inflexibility, loss of drive, complacency, and a tendency to look backward on past achievements rather than forward to future ones.

The company that has an awareness of the "internal" changes taking place in its work force and the potential erosive consequences of these changes is in a position to resolve this contradiction. It must first of all be recognized that there is no physical or biological reason for individuals to lose their effectiveness during their working years. The accumulation of work experience, the characteristics of steadiness and loyalty, the maturing process itself, should far outweigh in benefit any physical slowing down that takes place in the normal aging process among employees whose basic jobs are intellectual, technical, or otherwise skilled. (There is a view that in fields involving original research, scientific creativity diminishes with age. This may or may not be intrinsically true. It may seem to be the case because successful scientists and research engineers are often "rewarded" with management positions and thus naturally become more remote from their original fields of successful endeavor. In any event, even if true, this phenomenon would have to be considered special to the area of scientific research.)

The challenge to business managements is how to reap the benefits of maturity and experience that derive from a relatively stable work force without suffering the penalties of stagnation and complacency. To meet this challenge, managements must remind themselves that loyalty and steadiness are only two of the characteristics that define a valued employee. In addition, there is a continuing need to keep current and remain innovative. For technical and administrative personnel, this means attendance at work-related seminars, participation in continuing-education programs, refresher courses, subscriptions to journals, and any other activities that contribute new ideas and fresh viewpoints. For managers of lower-level personnel, this means in-house training programs to upgrade the capability of their work forces.

It is management's responsibility to provide reasonable financial support for individual self-improvement and to make available the time and direction for in-house training programs. The employee's responsibility is to take advantage of these opportunities. A survey of the number and kind of such programs sponsored by the company today and of the level of employee participation in them would provide a good indication of the directions toward which the company's vitality levels are trending.

QUANTITATIVE INDICES OF COMPANY VITALITY

The issues discussed in this chapter raise questions designed to enable the industrial firm to develop an approach to appraising its own vitality level. In-depth reviews of the various activities that have been discussed as well as others considered to be significant, if they are looked at from the standpoints of state of the art, innovative thrust, and follow-through power, should help the company's leaders form valid, qualitative judgments about the firm's overall energy level.

However, quantitative indices also may be developed and applied to strengthen the firm's self-appraisal capability in this important but elusive aspect of company life. The accompanying chart gives a brief description of a few of these possible indices. For any individual company, some of them may not be applicable. For all companies, additional ones would surely be useful. The measurements described are presented by way of suggestions. They represent an attempt to quantify some of the criteria that have been discussed earlier.

Each sample index is based upon comparison of current activity for the most recent full year with activity in the same function or program in previous years. If appropriate, and if sufficient data are available, an attempt should be made to project the level of activity one year ahead based on current planning information.

In most industrial firms, the data required to establish some of these indices are probably readily available and already being used for other purposes; for instance, share-of-the-market information and cost-reduction information. It is emphasized that they are included here only as part of a general program to appraise company vitality.

EMPLOYEE MOTIVATION AND COMPANY VITALITY

In this discussion, an attempt has been made to develop a tangible framework for an intangible idea—the idea of a vitality level as applied to organizations rather than individuals. The vitality level of an individual is a discernible aspect of his personality. The energetic, resilient person with a considerable concentration span is thought of as demonstrating a high level of vitality. Even among individuals, however, there are elusive elements in the energy levels that characterize them. This is so because psychological as well as physical factors determine the pace and the intensity of their lives. Many people who go through life with serious physical ailments, plagued by chronic illness, manage somehow to function at a pace that much healthier people are not able to sustain.

However, as hard as it is to evaluate the sources of vitality in individual human beings, it is even more difficult to apply this idea to complex business enterprises. What determines the pace of activity of a total organization comprising numerous individuals who range in temperament from phlegmatic to frenetic? Obviously, top management must set the general pace of activity for the total organization. But how is this management drive to be disseminated throughout the firm?

Perhaps this question can be dealt with by asking another question. "Why is there frequently such a disparity between the degree of psychic energy at the higher levels of the management pyramid and at the lower levels?" This is often asked self-righteously and in exasperation by business managers, but without their really seeking an answer. If the question is ever to be a useful and not merely a rhetorical one, an answer to it should be sought. The way to begin is, perhaps, by rephrasing the question in this way: "Why *does* top management care more about what is happening in the firm?" Here are some suggested answers:

1. Higher management levels control total organizations and visualize them as integrated units; therefore, it is easier for them to think of the enterprise in personal terms, to think of it as "theirs."

QUANTITATIVE INDICES OF COMPANY VITALITY

I. The Company Suggestion Plan
   A. Total number of suggestions proposed per year.
   B. Total number of suggestions implemented per year.
   C. Ratio of each of the above to the number of employees on the payroll qualified to participate in the program.
   D. Ratio of suggestions implemented to those proposed.
      Indication of the relative effectiveness of the program through time.
II. Product Improvement Record
   A. Number of product improvement ideas offered for each going product per year.
   B. Number of product improvement ideas implemented per product per year.
III. New Product Thrust
   A. Number of new products placed on the market per year.
      A longer time perspective is required for this index because of probable less frequency of occurrence, except for novelty firms or job shops.
   B. Number of new products in planning phase per year.
IV. Dollar Amount of Value Engineering Changes per Year
   A. Proposed.
   B. Implemented.
   C. Ratio of B to A.
   D. Relate B to appropriate base.
      Total cost of sales; sales.
V. Company Sales Share of the Market
   Broken down by region, product, and/or product line as appropriate and as available marketing data make possible.
VI. Net Fixed Investment after Depreciation by Year
   A declining trend may mean that plant and equipment are becoming less efficient or becoming obsolete, or that the company is unintentionally on a liquidation course. Even

a slowly accelerating trend of investment may be indicative of these conditions because of inflationary factors built into the price of capital items through time.

VII. Aging Process in the Firm

    A. Average age of technical (research and development) personnel through time.

    B. Average age of technical (manufacturing) personnel through time.

    C. Average age of administrative personnel through time.

    D. Average age of hourly personnel through time.

    "Aging" does not necessarily mean loss of company vitality. Experience plus innovative spirit can be a powerful combination. Aging accompanied by stagnation is obviously dangerous to a firm. This index should be used in combination with others.

VIII. Education Index

    A. Total number of post-high school years of schooling (including noncredit courses) of exempt employees divided by the number of exempt employees.

    This ratio may be broken down as appropriate by technical, nontechnical, and so on.

    B. Number of in-house training hours and outside seminar hours divided by number of employees.

    These ratios should be developed for categories of labor where state of the art is a vital factor.

IX. Vendor Turnover Index

    A. Number of new vendors adopted as a percentage of total vendors utilized.

    B. Percentage of purchase-dollar volume placed with new vendors as a percentage of total-dollar volume placed.

    A low percentage of vendor turnover is not necessarily a good or a bad condition. It could be an indication of a highly satisfactory relationship with suppliers. This ratio should be looked at in combination with the next one.

    C. Number of new vendors "shopped" per year as a percentage of total vendors used per year.

2. Outsiders regard top management as signifying the totality of the firm. The power of top management is recognized.

3. The psychological and material rewards given by the firm to higher management personnel are considerable.

The astute top management group can make the same factors that motivate them operative on some appropriate scale throughout the management pyramid:

1. It is true that all levels of management cannot control the total firm. But lower levels of management can be given an opportunity to control their piece of the organization within reasonable limits.

2. It is also true that lower levels of management cannot achieve the public prestige of top managers. But significant public recognition can be given to lower management personnel as well. For example, why not issue releases to the local or neighborhood press about the promotion of an assistant foreman to the position of foreman?

3. Appropriate internal recognition of outstanding performance by personnel at lower management levels conveys significant psychological rewards. Profit-sharing plans with broad and deep participation are an excellent means of identifying private economic interests with company interests.

The whole issue of psychic energy dissemination throughout the firm resolves itself to a question of management empathy. The top management group that asks the question "Why isn't the rest of the organization as well motivated as we are?" in a spirit of self-righteousness is missing the point. The question can be put to good use, however, if it is applied as a basis for establishing, to the extent feasible, similar incentives throughout the organization as are available at the top.

A FEW CLOSING WORDS

Once the basic criteria that define the nature and condition of the firm are brought into focus, the difficult task of managing complex organizations during periods of rapid social and economic change becomes easier. It has been the purpose of this book to combine these criteria into a single, unifying framework that can serve as the basis for a self-appraisal system for any business unit that needs to cope with the problems of complexity and change.

The unifying aspect of these self-appraisal criteria is their universality. Objectives, decision making for change, decision implementation, the operational-decision matrix, patterns of communication, psychic energy levels—these criteria are basic to the performance of all complex organizations. They are stable factors in even the most volatile of environments. The management group that keeps them in focus retains its ability to separate the important from the trivial. During these times when management groups are inundated with data to unparalleled extents, the ability to focus on essentials has become indispensable.

In each of the individual chapters dealing with the critical factors as self-appraisal indices, major problems were raised associated with each of them. In every case, approaches to solutions have been offered. It is hoped that these approaches will prove to be of value. But the main purpose both of raising troublesome questions and of proposing possible solutions has been to increase the awareness and the sensitivity of the reader to the essence of each of the basic criteria; in other words, to make the reader more introspective in terms of the nature and condition of his organization. To the extent that this is achieved, the author will feel that he has accomplished a useful purpose.

INDEX